Politics on Trial

Five Famous Trials of the 20th Century

a book in the Radical History series

radical history

radical historY

The massive anticapitalist protest movements storming our globe prove that people have not surrendered to the lie of the "end of history" or submitted to the ever-deadening, ever-demoralizing capitalist status quo.

Radical History, an exciting new series from Ocean Press, challenges the attempt to separate human beings from their histories and communities and reflects a confidence in humanity's capacity to change our society and ourselves.

Radical History seeks to revive events, struggles and people erased from conventional (and conservative) media and memory, providing invaluable resources for a new generation of political activists.

The series will include eyewitness accounts and historic, forgotten or ignored documents. It will publish speeches and articles as well as new essays, chronologies and further resources. These books are edited and designed by young political activists.

Series Editor: Deborah Shnookal

"We were born into an unjust system. We are not prepared to grow old in it."
–Bernadette Devlin

Politics on Trial

Five Famous Trials of the 20th Century

Introduction by Karin Kunstler Goldman, Michael Ratner and Michael Steven Smith

William Kunstler

Ocean Press
Melbourne ■ New York
www.oceanbooks.com.au

ISBN 1-876175-49-4

First printed 2003

Printed in Australia

Library of Congress Control Number 2002107120

Published by Ocean Press

Australia GPO Box 3279 Melbourne, Victoria 3001, Australia
          Tel 61 3 9326 4280
          Fax 61 3 9329 5040
          email: info@oceanbooks.com.au

USA   PO Box 1186 Old Chelsea Station, New York, NY 10113-1186, USA
          Tel 718 246 4160

Ocean Press Distributors

United States and Canada

Consortium
1045 Westgate Drive, Suite 90
Saint Paul, MN 55114-1065
1-800-283-3572

Britain and Europe

Global Book Marketing
38 King Street, London WC2E 8JT, UK
orders@globalbookmarketing.co.uk

Australia and New Zealand

Astam Books
57-61 John Street, Leichhardt, NSW 2040, Australia
info@astambooks.com.au

Cuba and Latin America

Ocean Press
Calle 21 #406, Vedado, Havana, Cuba

www.oceanbooks.com.au

Contents

Publisher's Note

The trials that are described in this book were major, public events in the United States in the 20th century. They capture the spirit of fear and political repression that has characterized dissidence in the United States. Many other trials could have been so described and it is hoped that this book may initiate a broader effort to record a more comprehensive range of political trials in the United States and elsewhere.

The five chapters in this book were first published in 1963 in the book *...And Justice for All*. The remaining five chapters from the original book, covering trials such as those of Tom Mooney and Alger Hiss, can be found at the website of the Radical History series: www.oceanbooks.com.au.

This book is dedicated to political prisoners past and present in the United States. The cases of Mumia Abu-Jamal and Leonard Peltier are symbolic of many other political activists jailed in the United States for their political beliefs and activity. They deserve our active solidarity.

A brief epilog to this book describes a more recent example of a political trial shaped by fear and intimidation. Five Cubans were jailed in Miami in 1998 and face extraordinary sentences for the "crime" of monitoring the activities of Miami-based terrorists who have a long record of attacks against sovereign Cuba. Their case highlights that the "war against terror" does not extend to others who seek to defend themselves from terror originating in the United States itself.

Bill Kunstler was an extraordinary individual. As a lawyer he championed the struggles of many and sought to expose the myths of democracy, justice and power in the United States. This book will be followed by another, larger volume that will collect many of the principal writings, speeches and interviews of Bill Kunstler.

Special thanks should be given to Karin Kunstler Goldman, Michael Ratner and Michael Steven Smith for their invaluable role in the preparation of *Politics on Trial*.

About the Editors

Karin Kunstler Goldman

Karin Kunstler Goldman is the eldest of Bill Kunstler's four daughters. She participated in the Mississippi Freedom Summer in 1964. Karin was a Peace Corps volunteer in Senegal from 1966 to 1968 and received a law degree from Rutgers University in 1973. Since 1982, she has been an assistant attorney general in the Charities Fraud division of the New York State Attorney General's office.

Michael Ratner

Michael Ratner is the president of the Center for Constitutional Rights in New York. He is intensely involved in challenging constitutional violations in the wake of 9/11. He has litigated numerous cases in the United States against major international human rights abusers, and has brought numerous challenges to U.S. war making in El Salvador, Nicaragua, Grenada, Iraq and Yugoslavia. He is currently teaching International Human Rights Litigation at Columbia Law School.

Michael Steven Smith

Michael Steven Smith, a law graduate of the University of Wisconsin, practises law in New York City where he is a member of the National Lawyers Guild. He is also member of the board of the New York Marxist School.

William Kunstler

"I've taken on a lot of pariahs. They may be local pariahs, like Martin Luther King in the South... or even up in Cicero, Illinois, because I think that the pariahs really set the course of U.S. civil liberties and civil rights... The pariahs get the rough treatment, for them the system violates every rule of ethics. We just had eight state troopers indicted in New York for moving a fingerprint card to a crime scene in order to implicate one of these pariah-type defendants. We know that they will violate the law every time in order to get a pariah.... So I think that the place for activist lawyers is with those people."

William Kunstler lived a long life in the public eye, fighting for social justice and combining political action with great personal courage. He maintained an unrelenting commitment and devotion to putting the criminal justice system on trial, even as he did his effective legal work inside a system he despised – where money buys justice and poverty goes to jail. Clearly, William Kunstler was one of the most important defense attorneys of this century. He was in a class with Clarence Darrow and few others and he lived on the cutting edge of radical history. A list of those he vigorously defended in nearly five decades as a brilliant courtroom strategist, committed to social justice and social change, includes H. Rap Brown, Martin Luther King Jr., Malcolm X, Marlon Brando, the 1,200 Attica Brothers, Jack Ruby and El Sayyid Nosair (accused of gunning down Jewish Defense League founder Rabbi Mayer Kahani). He was a history maker who impacted in a substantial way on the way we think about law and the waging of a legal defense.

"William Moses Kunstler died on Labor Day [1995] at age 76 of a heart attack. But I assure you it was a purely technical matter. He never lost hope, and the heart he brought to his work was huge, and was never lost to paralyzing bitterness or cynicism. Bill's good heart will go on beating in many of us for a long time to come." – Dennis Bernstein

"Fear... I use fear, and they don't teach you that in the Boy Scouts."

–Richard Nixon

Introduction

Karin Kunstler Goldman
Michael Ratner and
Michael Steven Smith

Richard Nixon, for whom William Kunstler had no respect, was once asked by a reporter what the secret of his political success was. "Fear," answered Nixon. "I use fear, and they don't teach you that in the Boy Scouts."

Because of the September 11, 2001, attack on the United States by political Islamists, fear is once again afoot in this country, just as it was in the 1950s when Nixon ascended on a chariot of anticommunism. Fear is again afoot as it was after World War I when anti-immigrant prejudice doomed Nicola Sacco and Bartolomeo Vanzetti, and as it was after World War II when anticommunist and anti-Semitic prejudice doomed Julius and Ethel Rosenberg.

This book is William Kunstler's explication of five key political trials, trials that helped shape U.S. politics and culture for much of the 20th century. Four of the defendants, Sacco and Vanzetti and the Rosenbergs, were executed in electric chairs. In *Alabama v. Patterson*, nine young African American men were framed and convicted for rape; they were victims of a ruthless racial prejudice infusing all levels of society. The trial of *Engel v. Vitale* took on those who fostered prayers to a Christian God in public schools, an issue which is still with us. It's corollary case, the Scopes trial in Tennessee, involved the suppression of the teaching of modern science. The issue of evolution, years later, is still passionately contended.

The evidence that (then trial lawyer) Kunstler deftly and succinctly summarizes does not support the verdicts rendered against the defendants. Although these cases were already historic landmarks when Kunstler set them out, he refrains from placing them in their historical context or from judging the defendants. He lets the trial testimonies speak for themselves. This is Bill's singular and powerful contribution.

All five of these trials were occasioned and sustained by communities infused with fear and prejudice, and as Roger Baldwin, a founder of the American Civil Liberties Union (ACLU), observed: "...how difficult it is for juries and judges to rise above community fears to deal justly and fairly with unpopular or hated defendants." In such a climate, laws that roll back the constitutional guarantees of the Bill of Rights are easily promulgated. We are facing just such a situation today in the wake of the September 11 attacks in the United States. Constitutional rights that most of us felt were sacrosanct no longer protect us; human rights protections guaranteed by international law have been disregarded.

The original title of this book "...And Justice For All" is, of course, ironic. The trials this book examines would not have taken place, much less resulted in convictions, if their instigators, prosecutors and jurors had held to the standards of the Pledge of Allegiance reprinted at the beginning of this book's original edition: "I pledge allegiance to the flag of the United States of America and to the republic for which it stands, one nation, under God, with liberty and justice for all."

When William Kunstler wrote the book in 1963 he was not yet the most well known, most effective, and to many, the most beloved lawyer in America. When he penned these chapters, Bill had not yet grown into his individual historic role, which would contribute to the making of that history. In 1963, he was a political liberal, a decorated veteran officer of World War II, and a married man with two children. He had a suburban home and was engaged in the general practice of law with his brother Michael — to whom his book was dedicated — in a small town outside of New York City. Intellectually accomplished, Bill graduated magna cum laude from Yale, in 1942, in French literature. He attained the rank of major, serving in the U.S. Army in the Pacific during the war, and then took a law degree at Columbia University, where he also taught English to undergraduates. Later, when he had become famous and was speaking on college campuses up to three or four times a week, he would flavor his talks with lines of favorite poems. Apart from Bill's literary background and analytical legal skills, he was an active participant in the ACLU, which was the main U.S. organization supporting the Bill of Rights, the first 10 amendments to the U.S. Constitution. Indeed, the ACLU's Roger Baldwin contributed the book's first introduction.

In 1963, however, Bill had not yet come to the understanding, as he expressed in a 1994 speech to the New York Association of Criminal Defense Lawyers, that the law "...is nothing other than a method of control created by a socioeconomic system determined, at all costs, to perpetuate itself by all and any means necessary, for as long as possible," or that the U.S. Supreme Court, the highest court in the land, is "...an enemy, a predominately white court representing the power structure." He came to this conclusion through his movement lawyering in the 1960s and through his extensive study of U.S. history.

After the 2001 terrorist attacks on the World Trade Center and the Pentagon, President George W. Bush announced, on national television and to great popular acclaim, a "war against terrorism" of indeterminate length and indefinable boundaries. "You are either with us or against us," Bush pronounced, assuring a traumatized U.S. public that God would not be neutral in this battle. Bush saw his personal popularity soar to unprecedented levels. Less than a year before it had taken a five to four vote of the reactionary U.S. Supreme Court to block a recount of the election ballots in Florida, installing Bush in office although he had garnered only a minority of the popular vote. In the 2000 elections, half the eligible voters did not even bother to turn out. Such, as Nixon advised, is the power of fear.

And so, the government has established a wide-ranging series of measures in its claimed effort to eradicate terrorism. Some of the key measures are analyzed further below. We have no doubt that Bill Kunstler would have been in the forefront of those opposed to these recent, draconian violations of law, which include the indefinite and arbitrary detention of battlefield detainees outside the standards of the Geneva Convention; military tribunals to try suspected terrorists; and the possible use of torture to obtain information. Bill would have led the fight against the massive arrest and interrogation of immigrants; against the passage of legislation granting intelligence and law enforcement agencies much broader powers to intrude into the private lives of U.S. citizens. He would have been especially incensed at recent new initiatives — such as the wiretapping of attorney-client conversations, or the FBI's new license to spy on domestic religious and political groups, or the undermining of core constitutional protections.

No book written by Bill Kunstler today would have omitted a discussion of the serious assault currently taking place in this country against people's rights, and particularly against the rights of those the state has selected for detention and/or prosecution.

The President's Military Order
a. Military Commissions

On November 13, 2001, President Bush signed a military order establishing military commissions or tribunals to try suspected terrorists. Under this order, noncitizens accused of aiding international terrorism, from the United States or elsewhere, can be tried before one of these commissions at the discretion of the president. These commissions are not court-martials, which provide far more protection for the accused.

The divergence from constitutional protections authorized by this executive order is breathtaking. In fact, Attorney General John Ashcroft has explicitly stated that terrorists do not deserve constitutional protection, and by "terrorists," Ashcroft also means accused or suspected individuals, not only those proven in any way to have committed terrorist acts. Accordingly, what have been established are essentially "courts" of conviction and not of justice.

Under the provisions of the military order establishing these commissions, the defense secretary is to appoint judges, most likely military officers, who will decide both questions of law and fact. Unlike federal judges who are appointed for life, these officers will have little independence and every reason to decide in favor of the prosecution. Normal rules of evidence, which provide some assurance of reliability, will not apply. Hearsay and even evidence obtained through torture will apparently be admissible. This is particularly alarming in light of the intimations from U.S. officials that torture of suspects may be an option.

The only appeal from a conviction will be to the president or the defense secretary. Incredibly, the entire process, including execution, can be carried out in secret and the trials can be held anywhere the defense secretary decides. A trial might occur on an aircraft carrier, for example, with no press allowed, and with the body of the executed disposed of at sea.

Although military tribunals were used during and immediately subsequent to World War II, their use since that time does not comply with important international treaties. The International Covenant on Civil and Political Rights as well as the UN Declaration of the Rights and Duties of Man, for example, require that persons be tried before courts previously established in accordance with preexisting laws. These tribunals are clearly not such courts. In addition, the Third Geneva Convention of 1949 requires that prisoners of war (POWs) be tried under the same procedures that U.S. soldiers would be tried under for similar crimes. U.S. soldiers are tried by courts-martial or civilian courts and never by military tribunal. This, most probably, is one important reason the United States has refused to classify the Guantánamo detainees as POWs; if they were POWs, the government would not be free to use tribunals.

The administration has claimed it will address some of these and other criticisms when regulations have been written. Still, as currently conceived, the president will select the defendants; the defense secretary will appoint the judges; the death penalty remains a sentencing option and no genuine appeal will be permitted.

Trials before military commissions will not be trusted in either the Muslim world or in Europe, where previous terrorism trials have not required the total suspension of the most basic principles of justice. The military commissions will be seen for what they are: "kangaroo courts."

b. Indefinite detention under military order; and the status of the Guantánamo prisoners

In addition to authorizing military tribunals, the same November 13, 2001, military order requires the defense secretary to detain anyone whom the president has reason to believe is an international terrorist; a member of al Qaeda; or anyone who has harbored such persons. There is no requirement that a detained individual ever be brought to trial. Detention without charges and without court review can potentially last a lifetime.

Subsequent to issuing the military order, U.S. and Northern Alliance forces in Afghanistan captured thousands of prisoners. On or about January 11, 2002, the U.S. military began transporting prisoners captured in Afghanistan to Camp X-Ray at the U.S. Naval Station in Guantánamo Bay, Cuba. As of April 2002, authorities were detaining 300 male prisoners representing over 30 nationalities at the Guantánamo compound, and the number was expected to grow. These prisoners may be indefinitely detained, to be tried by military tribunals at some indefinite point in the future. All of them potentially face the death penalty.

There have been allegations of the ill treatment of some prisoners, in transit and at Guantánamo, including reports that they were shackled, hooded and sedated during the 25-hour flight from Afghanistan; that their beards and heads were forcibly shaved; and that since arrival at Guantánamo they have been housed in small, cage-like cells that fail to protect against the elements. While such treatment is never acceptable, even more serious is the fact that these prisoners exist in a legal limbo; their identities remain secret; and the charges against them unknown.

It is the official position of the U.S. Government that none of these detainees are POWs. Instead, officials have repeatedly described the prisoners as "unlawful combatants." This determination was made without the convening of a competent tribunal as required by Article 5 of the Third Geneva Convention, which mandates such a tribunal "should any doubt arise" as to a combatant's status. In its most recent statement on the status of the Guantánamo detainees, the U.S. Government announced that although it would apply the Geneva Conventions to those prisoners it decided were from the Taliban, it would not extend them to prisoners it believed were members of al Qaeda. In no case, however, have any of those detained been considered POWs. The United States has repeatedly refused entreaties of the international community to treat all the detainees under the procedures established by the Geneva Conventions.

U.S. treatment of the Guantánamo detainees violates virtually every international human rights norm relating to preventive detention. The United States has denied the detainees access to counsel, consular representatives and family members; it has failed to notify them of the charges they are facing; and has refused to allow for judicial review of the detentions. It has expressed its intent to hold the detainees indefinitely into the future.

FBI Arrests and Investigations

a. Arrests of noncitizens

The FBI has always done more than chase criminals; like the CIA it has long considered itself the protector of U.S. ideology. In the past, those who have opposed government policies — civil rights workers, anti-Vietnam war protestors, opponents of the covert Reagan-era wars, or cultural dissidents — have repeatedly been subject to surveillance and had their legal activities disrupted by the FBI.

In the immediate aftermath of the September 11 attacks, Attorney General Ashcroft focused FBI efforts on noncitizens, whether permanent residents, students, temporary workers or tourists. Previous to September 11, an alien could only be held for 48 hours prior to the filing of charges. Ashcroft's new regulation allows arrested aliens to be held, without charges, for a "reasonable time" — presumably months or longer.

The FBI began massive detentions and investigations of individuals suspected of terrorist connections, almost all of them non-U.S. citizens of Middle Eastern descent. Over 1,300 people were arrested. In some cases, they were arrested merely for being from a country such as Pakistan and having expired student visas. Many were held for weeks and months without access to lawyers and with no knowledge of the charges against them; many are still in detention. None, as yet, have been proven to have a connection with the September 11 attacks; most remain in jail despite any links to terrorism having been cleared. Stories of the mistreatment of such detainees are common.

Some of those arrested are unwilling, apparently, to talk to the FBI, though in return they have been offered shorter jail sentences, jobs, money and new identities. Astonishingly, the FBI and the Justice Department have discussed methods to force them to talk, which include "using drugs or pressure tactics such as those employed by Israeli interrogators."[1] The accurate term to describe these tactics is torture.

As torture is illegal in the United States and under international law, U.S. officials risk lawsuits by using such practices. For this reason, they have suggested using another country to do their dirty work; they want to extradite the suspects to allied countries where security services regularly threaten family members and/or use torture. It would be difficult to imagine a more ominous signal of the repressive period we are facing.

b. Investigations of Middle Eastern men and of dissenters

In late November 2001, Ashcroft announced that the FBI and other law enforcement personnel would interview more than 5,000 men, mostly from the Middle East, who were in the United States on temporary visas. None of these men were suspected of any crime. The interviews were supposedly voluntary. A number of civil liberties organizations, Muslim and Arab American groups objected that the investigations amounted to racial profiling and that interviews of immigrants who might be subject to deportation could hardly be called voluntary. A number of law enforcement officials, including a former head of the FBI, objected as well, saying that such questioning would harm the relationship of police departments with minority communities; that the practice was illegal under some state laws and that it was a clumsy and ineffective way to go about an investigation. A few local police departments refused to cooperate.

Although Ashcroft claimed the questioning was harmless, the questions themselves made this assertion doubtful. Initial questions concerned the noncitizen's status — if there was even the hint of a technical immigration violation, the person could well find himself in jail and deported. Information was requested regarding all of the friends and family members of the questioned person; in other words, the FBI wanted complete address books. Once the FBI had such information, it would open files and investigations on each of those named, even though no one was suspected of a crime.

Other questions concerned whether the person interviewed had any sympathy with any of the causes supposedly espoused by the attackers on September 11. Media reports in this country and elsewhere have suggested, for example, that the attackers were acting in the name of Palestinian rights. Whether or not this is the case, many Arab Americans are sympathetic with the plight of the Palestinians, and would be put in a bind by FBI questioning about this topic. If the person questioned by the FBI admitted to such sympathy he would immediately become a potential suspect; if he was sympathetic, but denied it, he would be lying to the FBI, which is a federal crime.

The FBI was instructed to make informants of the persons it questioned, and to have them continue to report on and monitor the people they are in contact with. The FBI is also currently investigating political dissident groups it claims are linked to terrorism — among them pacifist groups such as the U.S. chapter of Women in Black, which holds peaceful vigils to protest violence in Israel and the Palestinian Territories. The FBI has threatened to force members of Women in Black to either talk about their group or go to jail. As one of the group's members said, "If the FBI cannot or will not distinguish between groups who collude in hatred and terrorism, and peace activists who struggle in the full light of day against all forms of terrorism, we are in serious trouble."[2]

The FBI, unfortunately, does not make that distinction. We face not only the roundup of thousands on flimsy suspicions, but also an all-out investigation of dissent in the United States.

c. Renewed FBI spying on religious and political groups

John Ashcroft is considering a plan that would authorize the FBI to spy upon and disrupt political groups.[3] This spying and disruption would take place even without evidence that a group was involved in anything illegal. A person or group could become a target solely because of expressing views different from those of the government or taking a position opposing, for example, U.S. foreign policy in the Middle East.

Ashcroft would authorize this by lifting FBI guidelines that were put into place in the 1970s after abuses of the agency were exposed, under a program called Cointelpro, or "Counterintelligence Program," which existed to "misdirect, discredit, disrupt and otherwise neutralize" specific individuals and groups. Probably the most notorious goal of Cointelpro was the FBI's effort to prevent the rise of what it called a "Black Messiah," which included for example, spying upon and disrupting the activities of Dr. Martin Luther King. It is still unknown whether this proposed new version of Cointelpro has been adopted.

Attorney-Client Communications

At the heart of the effective assistance of counsel is the right of a criminal defendant to a lawyer with whom he or she can communicate, candidly and freely, without fear that the government will overhear confidential communications. This right is fundamental to the adversarial system of justice in the United States, flawed as it is, as Kunstler came to believe. When the government overhears such conversations, a defendant's right to a defense is compromised. With the stroke of a pen, Attorney General Ashcroft has now eliminated the attorney-client privilege and will wiretap privileged communications when he thinks there is "reasonable suspicion to believe" that a detainee "may use communications with attorneys or their agents to further facilitate an act or acts of violence or terrorism."[4] Ashcroft has said that approximately 100 suspects and their attorneys may be subject to the order. He claims the legal authority to do so without court order, without the approval and finding by a neutral magistrate that attorney-client communications are facilitating criminal conduct. This is utter lawlessness by our country's top law enforcement officer and is, without doubt, unconstitutional.

The New Antiterrorist Legislation

On October 26, 2001, sweeping new antiterrorist legislation was signed by President Bush and passed by Congress. The USA Patriot Act (Uniting and Strengthening America by Providing Appropriate Tools Required to Intercept and Obstruct Terrorism), was aimed at both aliens and citizens. The legislation met more opposition than one might expect in these difficult times. Over 120 groups ranging from the right to the left, formed a National Coalition to Protect Political Freedom, to oppose the worst aspects of the proposed new law. They succeeded in making minor modifications, but the most troubling provisions remain, and are described below:

a. "Rights" of aliens

Prior to this legislation, antiterrorist laws passed in the wake of the 1996 bombing of the federal building in Oklahoma, had already given the government wide powers to arrest, detain and deport aliens based upon secret evidence — that neither the alien nor his attorney could view or refute. The new legislation makes it even worse for aliens. First, the law permits "mandatory detention" of aliens certified by the attorney general as "suspected terrorists." These could include people involved in all types of activity — from bar room brawls to those who have provided humanitarian assistance only to organizations disliked by the United States. Once certified in this way, an alien could be imprisoned indefinitely with no real opportunity for court challenge. Until now, such "preventive detention" was believed to be categorically unconstitutional.

Second, current law permits deportation of aliens who support terrorist activity; the proposed law would make aliens deportable for almost any association with a "terrorist organization." Even if this change seems to have a certain surface plausibility, it represents a dangerous erosion of the constitutionally protected rights of association. "Terrorist organization" is a broad and open-ended term that could, depending on the political climate or the inclinations of the attorney general, include liberation groups such as the Irish Republican Army, the African National Congress, or NGOs that have ever engaged in any violent activity, such as Greenpeace. An alien who gives only medical or humanitarian aid to similar groups, or simply supports their political message in a material way, could also be jailed indefinitely.

b. More powers to the FBI and CIA

A key element in the USA Patriot Act is the wide expansion of wiretapping. In the United States wiretapping is permitted, but generally only when there is probable cause to believe a crime has been committed and a judge has signed a special wiretapping order that specifies limited time periods, the numbers of the telephones wiretapped and the type of conversations that will be overheard.

In 1978, an exception was made to these strict requirements, permitting wiretapping to be carried out to gather intelligence information about foreign governments and foreign "terrorist" organizations. A secret court was established, the Foreign Intelligence Surveillance Court, that could approve such wiretaps without requiring the government to show evidence of criminal conduct. In doing so, constitutional protections supposedly guarded throughout the investigation of crimes, could be bypassed.

The secret court has been little more than a rubber stamp for wiretapping requests by the spy agencies. It has authorized over 13,000 wiretaps in its 22-year existence, currently about a thousand last year, and apparently has never denied a request for a wiretap. Under the new law, the same secret court will have the power to authorize wiretaps and secret searches of homes in domestic criminal cases — not just to gather foreign intelligence. The FBI will be able to wiretap individuals or organizations without meeting the stringent requirements of the U.S. Constitution, which requires a court order based upon probable cause that a person is planning or has committed a crime. The new law authorizes the secret court to permit roving wiretaps of any phones, computers or cell phones that might possibly be used by a suspect. Widespread reading of e-mail will be allowed, even before the recipient opens it. Thousands of conversations will be heard or read that have nothing to do with any suspect or any crime.

The new legislation overflows with many other expansions of investigative and prosecutorial power, including wider use of undercover agents to infiltrate organizations, longer jail sentences, lifetime supervision for some who have served their sentences, more crimes that can receive the death penalty and longer statutes of limitations for prosecuting crimes. Another provision of the new bill makes it a crime for a person to fail to notify the FBI if he or she has "reasonable grounds to believe" that someone is about to commit a terrorist offense. The language of this provision is so vague that any person, however innocent, with any connection to any other person only remotely suspected of being a terrorist, can be prosecuted.

The New Crime of Domestic Terrorism

The USA Patriot Act creates a number of new crimes. The crime of "domestic terrorism" is one of the most threatening to those who oppose government policies and to dissent in general. Domestic terrorism is loosely defined as acts that are dangerous to human life, violate criminal law and "appear to be intended" to "intimidate or coerce a civilian population" or "influence the policy of a government by intimidation of coercion." Under this definition, for example, the

1999 demonstrations in Seattle against globalization and the World Trade Organization could fit within the classification.

What an unnecessary addition to the criminal code! There are already plenty of laws that make such civil disobedience criminal, without labeling protest as "terrorism" and imposing severe prison sentences.

Overall, the severe curtailment of legal rights, the disregard for established law and the new repressive legislation, represent one of the most sweeping assaults on our liberties in the last 50 years. It is unlikely to make us more secure; it is certain to make us less free. In times of war or national crisis, it is common for governments to reach for draconian law enforcement solutions. It has happened often in the United States and elsewhere. We should learn from historical example. Times of hysteria, war and instability are not times to rush to enact new laws that curtail our freedoms and grant more authority to the government and its intelligence and law enforcement agencies.

The U.S. Government has conceptualized the war against terrorism as a permanent war, a war without boundaries. Terrorism is frightening to all of us, but it is equally chilling to think that in the name of antiterrorism the U.S. government is willing to permanently suspend constitutional freedoms.

Today, "antiterrorism" has replaced the anticommunism of the 1950s and the anti-immigrant scare campaign of the 1920s as the ideology in service to reaction. "Antiterrorism" facilitated the U.S. Government's ability to increase the "defense" budget by $38 billion. The increase itself represents more money spent on arms than any other country on the planet.

Bad schools, poor or no health care, a devastated environment, huge under- and unemployment, all these have taken a back seat in the "war on terrorism." The government's refusal to even address such social problems has been necessarily in tandem with the enormous rollback in civil liberties sketched above.

William Kunstler often spoke of the example of the German government between the wars, when at that point of no return, the

Weimar Republic turned fascist. We are not alarmist, but our fear of a neofascism taking root in the United States is not ill-grounded or ahistorical. Long strides in that direction have been taken in the aftermath of the September 11 attacks, and many in the United States buy into the false proposition that their security rests on the giving up of certain democratic rights.

Bill Kunstler, reflecting on the U.S. Government's crushing of Black Panther activists in the 1960s, wrote "...the shadow of the swastika is still only dimly visibly on the walls that loom about our trembling heads. The key to survival, of course, is to be able to hear the booted tread before it stops in front of your own door." Truly the worst thing we have to fear, is fear itself, for as the cases outlined in this volume attest — democracy and its guarantees can come unraveled very quickly.

New York
May 1, 2002

---

[1] Walter Pincus, "Silence of 4 Terror Probe Suspects Poses Dilemma," *Washington Post* (October 21, 2001) A6

[2] Report by Ronnie Gilbert, FBI Investigation of Women in Black, October 4, 2001, at www.labournet.net/world/0110/wmnblk1.html

[3] David Johnston and Don Van Natta Jr., "Ashcroft Seeking to Free F.B.I. to Spy on Groups," *New York Times* (Dec. 1, 2001) A1

[4] National Security; Prevention of Terrorist Acts of Violence, 28 CFR Parts 500 and 501.

Sacco & Vanzetti

Massachusetts v. Bartolomeo Vanzetti and Nicola Sacco

The arrests of Nicola Sacco and Bartomoleo Vanzetti coincided with a period of intense political repression in the United States, the "Red Scare" of 1919-20. Charged with robbery and first degree murder, the two Italian-born immigrants were eventually convicted, in the face of evidence of perjured testimonies by prosecution witnesses, illegal activities by the police and a confession to the crime by a convicted bank robber.

While neither Sacco nor Vanzetti had any previous criminal record, they were long recognized by the authorities and their communities as anarchist militants who had been extensively involved in labor strikes, political agitation and antiwar propaganda. They were also known to be dedicated supporters of Luigi Galleani's Italian-language journal *Cronaca Sovversiva*, the most influential anarchist journal in the United States. In the unsafe atmosphere of those times, the two men initially lied to police, whose questioning focused on their radical activities and not on the specifics of the crime. Much of their defense then focused on whether those initial lies proved Sacco and Vanzetti's involvement in the crime or whether their understandable attempt to conceal their radicalism (and the identity of their friends) signified instead a time of national hysteria directed mainly toward foreign-born radicals.

On April 9, 1927, after all recourse in the Massachusetts courts had failed, Sacco and Vanzetti were sentenced to death. By then, the

dignity and the words of the two men, who proclaimed their innocence until the end, had turned them into powerful symbols of social
justice for many throughout the world. On August 23, 1927, a date
that has since become a watershed in 20th century U.S. history, the
two anarchists were executed in the electric chair.

Fifty years later, in 1997, the governor of Massachusetts, Michael
Dukakis, issued a public statement conceding that the atmosphere of
Sacco and Vanzetti's trial and appeals were "permeated by prejudice
against foreigners and hostility toward unorthodox political views;"
that "the conduct of many officials involved in the case sheds serious
doubt on their willingness and ability to conduct the prosecution and
trial of Sacco and Vanzetti fairly and impartially;" and that "the trial
and execution of Sacco and Vanzetti should serve to remind all civi-
lized people of the constant need to guard against our susceptibility
to prejudice, our intolerance of unorthodox ideas and our failure
to defend the rights of persons who are looked upon as strangers in
our midst."

Karin Kunstler

Thursday, April 15, 1920, dawned bright and windy in South
Braintree, Massachusetts, a manufacturing town some 20 miles south
of Boston. Shortly after 9:00 that morning, Shelley A. Neal, the local
U.S. Express agent, waited at the New Haven railroad station for the
delivery of a $15,776.51 payroll. The money was consigned to Slater
& Morrill, Inc., one of South Braintree's two shoe companies.

The cash arrived on the Boston train at about 9:10 a.m., and Neal
took it to his office on the first floor of Hampton House, a four-story
building on Railroad Avenue, a few feet from its intersection with
Pearl Street — South Braintree's main thoroughfare. Slater &
Morrill occupied the top three floors of Hampton House, with its
business office on the second floor. After he had sorted and counted the money, Neal left his office and walked down Railroad Avenue
to the shoe company's main entrance in the center of the rectangu-
lar building. As he locked his door, he saw that the hands on his
office clock stood at exactly 9:30 a.m. He was a rapid walker and had
almost arrived at the double-doored entrance before he noticed,
with some apprehension, that a large, newly varnished black automobile with its motor running was parked alongside the curb.

When Neal passed the car, he saw that its driver, a light-haired
man with an emaciated, jaundiced face, was watching him intently.
As he entered Hampton House, he observed that the man got into

the car and drove slowly up Railroad Avenue. Neal followed the vehicle with his eyes and thought that he could glimpse another man sitting in its rear seat. Although he later admitted that he had considered the driver's conduct extremely suspicious, the agent did not report the incident to anyone at Slater & Morrill.

The company's paymistress receipted for the money and began at once to fill the pay envelopes. When she had finished, the grey-colored packets were stacked in two large flat tins. Thursday was payday at the factory, and the boxes were scheduled to be picked up at 3:00 that afternoon by Frederick A. Parmenter, Slater & Morrill's acting paymaster.

The car that had aroused Neal's suspicions was apparently seen in other parts of South Braintree that morning. At 10:30 a.m., Harry E. Dolbeare, a piano repairman, was walking on Hancock Street when he noticed what he later described as "a carload of foreigners" in a large black sedan turning into Hancock Street from Holbrook Avenue. In the back of the car, he saw a man with "a very heavy mustache... leaning forward as though he was talking to either the driver or the other person in front of the car." In all, there were four men in the car who appeared to him to be "a tough looking bunch."

A little after 11:30 a.m., Mrs. Lola R. Andrews, an unemployed practical nurse, arrived in South Braintree with Mrs. Julia Campbell, an elderly friend. Both women were seeking work and applied first at Slater & Morrill's Factory No. 2, another four-story frame building which was located about an eighth of a mile east of Hampton House on Pearl Street. As the women entered the factory, Mrs. Andrews noticed a large black car parked in front of it. She saw a swarthy man, dressed in dark clothing, bending over the hood. In the back seat, she observed a thin, emaciated looking man with what she later depicted as "a light complexion."

There were no jobs open at Slater & Morrill and, when Mrs. Andrews left the building some 15 minutes later, she saw that the swarthy man was now lying on the ground with his head and shoulders under the front part of the vehicle. The sickly looking man, who had been sitting in the rear seat, was outside, leaning against the back of the car. Mrs. Andrews asked the man under the car if he could direct her to the Rice & Hutchins factory. At the sound of her voice, he got to his feet and pointed to the five-story brick building which was some 120 ft. west of Factory No. 2.

Earlier that day, John M. Faulkner, a Cohasset pattern maker who was bound for the hospital at the Watertown Arsenal to be treated for an infected hand, had boarded the 9:20 a.m. train to Boston. He was sitting in the second seat on the left hand side of the smoker. As the train came into East Weymouth, the passenger sitting on his right asked him if the stop was East Braintree. As Faulkner remembered it: "He said, 'the man behind me wants to know if it is East Braintree.' " The pattern maker had then looked at the other man who was sitting in a single seat near the lavatory. "He looked like a foreigner, with a black mustache, and cheekbones." The "foreigner" wore a felt hat and was dressed in "kind of old clothes." Faulkner had watched him leave the train, carrying a leather bag, when the local pulled into East Braintree shortly after 10:00 a.m.

At 11:30 a.m., William S. Tracy, a real estate broker, had driven by South Braintree Square. He "saw two men standing with their backs against the window of that drugstore, the window nearest the corner of Pearl Street." Some 10 minutes later, he returned to the square and noticed that the two strangers were still there. "The man nearest the drugstore was the shorter of the two and the other fellow... the shorter man of the two, he stood erect, and their general appearance was that they were dressed respectably and looked as if they might have been waiting for a car." What had attracted his attention to the men, whom he thought were Italians, was the fact that "no one was allowed to lean up against that building."

Just after noon, one William J. Heron, a railroad detective, saw two strange men loitering near the station restroom. "One of them was about 5 ft. 6 inches, weighed about 145 pounds, Italian. The other fellow was about 5 ft. 11; I should say, weighed about 160. They were smoking cigarettes, one of them." He had observed them closely because he considered it unusual for them to be there with no train due for some time, and "they acted kind of funny to me, nervous..." Heron had come to South Braintree looking for a lost boy whom he had found in the station and taken into the ticket office. When he emerged, a few minutes later, "the two men were gone."

Shortly before 3:00 p.m., Frederick Parmenter and Alessandro Berardelli, a guard, arrived at the paymistress's office on the second floor of Hampton House. They signed for the payroll and each man took one of the tin boxes containing the pay envelopes. Mark Carrigan, a shoe cutter who worked on the third floor of Hampton House, watched the two men leave the building. They crossed Railroad Avenue, passed to the right of the New Haven station, talked briefly with James E. Bostock, a Slater & Morrill millwright, and then started up Pearl Street toward Factory No. 2.

A few minutes earlier, Bostock had noticed two foreign looking strangers — he later said he thought they were Italian fruit peddlers — leaning against a fence near a water tank on the north side of Pearl Street, but he did not mention them to Parmenter or Berardelli. His conversation with the paymaster and the guard was brief — he remembered only that Parmenter had ordered him to "go into the other factory and fix the pulley on the motor" and that he had answered that he couldn't do the job that afternoon because he was "going to get this quarter past three car to Brockton."

Albert Frantello, a former Slater & Morrill employee, also saw the two strangers who had attracted Bostock's attention, and remembered that "the one that was nearest me had on a black cap, dark suit, dirty front on him, looked like a jersey, dark complexion and needed a shave, and he was a stocky build. The other fellow, he was light complexioned. He had on a cap and a dark suit. He was about as tall as the other fellow, same height, only he was slimmer, kind of pale looking, and his hair was light. He was not a stocky build." The first man had been wearing "a dark cap... pulled down just like any ordinary fellow would have his cap on, just resting on his forehead." The two men had been having an argument and Frantello overheard the stocky one berate his companion "in the American language."

After his brief conversation with Parmenter and Berardelli, Bostock hurried on toward Hampton House. He had only gone a few steps when he was startled to hear a fusillade of shots behind him. He turned and saw the guard Berardelli lying on the ground and a man standing over him with a smoking pistol in his hand. As he later testified, "...he stood over him. He shot, I should say, he shot at Berardelli probably four or five times. He stood guard over him." Parmenter had dropped his box when he was hit by the first bullet and managed to run across Pearl Street, closely pursued by a second man who shot him in the back just as the pair reached an excavation for a new restaurant on the north side of the street.

According to Bostock, both bandits "was dressed in sort of dark clothes, with... dark caps... they appeared to be foreigners." As for their physical appearance, "they was fellows of medium build... smooth face, dark complexioned." When one of the gunmen fired two shots at him, the millwright jumped behind the wooden fence, where he had first noticed them just before meeting Parmenter and

Berardelli. He had started to run back toward the railroad crossing when a black seven-passenger Buick drove slowly down the street, picked up the two gunmen and their loot, the tin boxes, and then proceeded down Pearl Street toward the railroad crossing. The mill-wright ducked behind the water tank as the car shot by him. It was so close to him that, "if I laid out at arm's length I could have touched the spokes of the car as it passed me." He saw four men inside, one of whom was firing at the excited crowd which was rap-idly collecting around the bodies of the paymaster and the guard.

When the shooting started, Lewis L. Wade, a sole leather cutter who doubled in brass as an auto mechanic for Slater & Morrill, was filling Mr. Slater's car with gasoline from a pump located in a little concrete shed in front of Factory No. 2. He saw Parmenter run across the street and disappear from view behind "a dirt truck." A short, bareheaded man who "needed a shave" was standing over Berardelli, pumping bullets into the fallen guard. "And the next thing that I saw was a car come up Pearl Street, and stop — well, it didn't exactly stop. I wouldn't say for sure whether it stopped or not. And there was a man at the wheel... he was a pale-faced man, I should judge... about probably 30 or 35. He looked to me like a man that had sickness... he was sick."

As soon as the car had passed him, Wade ran into the factory office and called in the first alarm to the Braintree police. When he returned, he "went to where Berardelli lay, and he was not dead then. He was breathing, and when he breathed the blood would come up and down on his face." Across the street, the mechanic noticed that James E. McGlone, a teamster who was transporting stone from the restaurant excavation, was struggling to keep his frightened team from stampeding. McGlone later described the killers as "dark-skinned Italians" while Hans Behrsin, Mr. Slater's chauffeur, who had been crouched behind the gasoline shed during the shooting, thought they had been "light complexioned boys."

Mrs. Barbara Liscomb, who had been looking out on Pearl Street from a third-floor window squarely in the middle of the Rice & Hutchins building, said she saw "two men lying on the ground and one man, a short, dark man, standing on the ground facing me with his head up, holding a revolver in his hands." She was only at the win-dow "about two seconds," having collapsed when the man waved the gun at her, and she did not see the automobile traveling down Pearl Street. As she later put it, "I sort of fainted away."

Mary E. Splaine, a Slater & Morrill bookkeeper, was working in her corner office on the second floor of Hampton House that afternoon. Just after 3:00 p.m., she had watched Parmenter and Berardelli walk up Pearl Street toward Factory No. 2, and had returned to her desk when they passed out of her line of vision. When she heard the shots, which she first thought were automobiles backfiring, she returned to the windows which opened on Pearl Street. She saw a black automobile driving slowly in the direction of the railroad tracks. It crossed the tracks and, as it passed under her window, she saw one of its passengers leaning out of the car, a man she later described as "an active looking man."

Miss Splaine did not see the actual shooting but 22-year-old Lewis Pelser, a Rice & Hutchins employee, claimed that he did. He was working on the main floor of the factory building when he heard the first shots. He had rushed to the window, looked out and, as he put it, "I seen this fellow shoot this fellow. It was the last shot. He put four bullets into him." The killer "had wavy hair pushed back, very strong hair, wiry hair, very dark." Pelser also jotted down the license number of the car, noticing as he did so that the rear window of the vehicle had been removed and that a rifle or shotgun barrel protruded from this opening. Edgar C. Langlois, his foreman, had watched the shooting from the floor above Pelser. According to him, the murderers had been "stout... thick-chested young men."

Winifred H. Pierce, a Slater & Morrill shoemaker, had run to a window on the Pearl Street side of Hampton House as soon as the gunplay started. He saw two men in a black car, one of whom was climbing into the front seat from the rear. Lawrence D. Ferguson, a coworker who was standing next to Pierce at the window, corroborated his story. But Daniel J. O'Neil, a South Braintree school boy, had a different version. According to him, the man in the car's back seat had "walked along [its] running board and before the car had got over the other side of the crossing that man was sitting in the front seat." The man he had seen "was a man [with] dark hair, cleanly shaven, broad shoulders... of light complexion... He wore a blue suit and no hat and his hair was thick but light and combed back straight over his head."

As Parmenter and Berardelli walked up Pearl Street toward Factory No. 2, they had been followed by Roy E. Gould, a razor sharpening paste peddler, who hoped to sell his product to the Slater & Morrill employees after they were paid. He was running in order to get to the factory before the paymaster did, so that he could set up his display stand. Before he could catch up with the two men, the hold-up occurred. As the Buick passed within 10 feet of him on its way toward the railroad crossing, one of the gunmen fired at him, the bullet piercing the pocket of his overcoat without injuring him. Gould gave his name to a Braintree policeman and indicated that he would be available for questioning if needed. His observations apparently failed to titillate the police and he was never questioned by them.

Frank J. Burke, an itinerant glassblower who had arrived in South Braintree at 2:30 that afternoon to give a demonstration of his art at a local school, claimed that the hold-up car had passed within 10 feet of him after the shooting. When he first saw it, the sedan was moving slowly down Pearl Street toward the railroad crossing. He watched two men jump on the running board and climb into the back seat. As the car approached the crossing, one of these men crawled into the front seat next to the driver. Seconds later, Burke heard a gunshot in the car, and the man who had climbed over into the front seat pointed a revolver at him and shouted, "Get out of the way, you son of a bitch!" He saw "a dark man with a short cropped mustache" in the rear of the car.

Mark Carrigan watched the car drive over the Pearl Street crossing but it was going too fast for him to recognize anyone in it. One of its occupants, "had black hair and looked, possibly, like an Italian." Louis De Beradinis, who owned a shoe repair shop at the corner of Railroad Avenue and Pearl Street, noticed a man with a gun standing on the vehicle's running board. "This man pointed a revolver to my face" and he had "a long face, awful white, and light hair combed in the back. It was a thin fellow I saw."

Carlos E. Goodridge, a Victrola salesman, who was whiling away a slow day in Magazu's poolroom which was a block west of Hampton House on the north side of Pearl Street, rushed out when he heard the excitement. He saw the black sedan cross the New Haven tracks and watched, with idle curiosity, as it approached Magazu's. Suddenly, he noticed that one of its occupants — "a dark complexioned fellow, with dark hair, a peculiar face that came down pointed" — was pointing a gun at him, and he jumped back into the poolroom and hid under one of the tables.

Michael Levangie, the gate tender at the Pearl Street crossing, had lowered his gates for an approaching train when the Buick came toward him. He was startled to see that one of the passengers in the car was pointing a revolver at his head. He was ordered by this man to raise his gates. He remembered that the person who shouted at him spoke with a decided foreign accent, although it was Burke's recollection that the man who ordered him out of the way had used good English. As Levangie later testified, "I looked back at the train to see if I had a chance to let them go. I saw that there was a chance, and I put my gates back where they belonged." He was able to describe only one of the vehicle's occupants, the driver, who, he said, was "a dark complexioned man with cheekbones sticking out, black hair, heavy brown mustache, slouch hat and army coat."

The Buick continued down Pearl Street and turned left on Hancock Street. As it crossed the New Haven tracks, it was seen by eight railroad workers, most of whom described the driver as "kind of light-complexioned" and the man sitting alongside of him on the front seat as "big and dark." Shelley Neal saw it make the turn when he ran out of his office upon hearing the shots. As it passed the drugstore on the corner of Pearl and Hancock, its passengers scattered rubber-headed tacks along the road. It took more than a week before South Braintree could count a day without at least one blowout on Hancock Street. Daniel Buckley, a railroad employee, was the last person in South Braintree to see the car as it headed out of town on South Street.

Several people remembered spotting it later that afternoon as it headed south through Randolph, Canton, Stoughton, Brockton and West Bridgewater. At 4:00 p.m., 16-year-old Julie Kelliher, a student at Brockton's Hancock School, saw a black sedan hurtling through that town at such a high rate of speed that she reported it to the police. It was next seen by Austin Reed, the gate tender at the Matfield Crossing just outside of West Bridgewater, at 4:15 p.m., Reed waved his warning sign at the oncoming automobile because a train was expected momentarily. One of the men in the car pointed his finger at the startled gate tender and snarled, "What to hell you hold us up for?" The man he saw was "a dark complexioned man, with kind of hollow cheeks, high cheekbones, had a stubby mustache. His hair was black."

Meanwhile, back in South Braintree, the horror-struck bystanders, who had been scattered momentarily by some shots from the rear window of the disappearing Buick, regathered around the two wounded men. Berardelli was lying in the street with his head next to the curbing. He was almost dead. According to Jim Bostock, the first man to reach him, "[Berardelli] laid in a kind of crouched position and I helped lay him down and every time he breathed, blood flowed and was coming out of his mouth." The two men were taken to the home of Horace A. Colbert, a railroad tower man who lived just east of the restaurant excavation, where Berardelli died. Parmenter lived until 5:00 the next morning.

Fred L. Loring, a Slater & Morrill shoe worker, noticed a cap with earlaps near Berardelli's body, which he picked up and turned over to his superintendent. The next day, the latter gave the cap to Jeremiah F. Gallivan, Braintree's police chief, who kept it under the seat of his car for 10 days before delivering it to Brockton's Captain John Scott. The only other evidence found at the scene were some empty cartridges which littered Pearl Street. Berardelli's Harrington & Richardson revolver, which he had been carrying that day, was missing.

Two days later, the Buick was discovered by two horsemen in Bridgewater's Manley Woods, some five miles west of the Matfield Crossing. Leading away from the abandoned vehicle were the tire-tracks of a smaller car. Although the black sedan's license tags had been removed, plates with the number which Louis Pelser had jotted down two days before had been pilfered from another car early in 1920. The Buick itself had been reported as stolen by its owner, a Dr. Francis J. Murphy, on November 23, 1919. The glass rear window was pushed out and there was a bullet hole in the car's right rear interior. It was later identified by almost every eyewitness as similar to the one they had seen on the day of the robbery.

Bridgewater's Police Chief Michael E. Stewart was convinced that the crime had been committed by a resident Italian who owned a car. Mike Boda, who boarded with a radical named Coacci in a shack near the Manley Woods, was interviewed by Stewart three days after the South Braintree murders. He told the police officer that his car, a small Overland, was stored in Simon Johnson's garage in West Bridgewater. Stewart called on Johnson and told him to notify the police if anyone called for Boda's car.

On the evening of May 5, Nicola Sacco, a Stoughton shoe worker; Bartolomeo Vanzetti, a Plymouth fish peddler; Boda and a mutual friend named Ricardo Orciani, started out from the former's house for West Bridgewater to pick up the Overland. Sacco and Vanzetti took the trolley while the other two men rode on Orciani's motorcycle. When Boda and Orciani arrived at the garage, they found it locked. They then walked over to Johnson's house where they were soon joined by Sacco and Vanzetti. Boda rang the bell and, when the garage owner's wife opened the door, told her that he had come for the Overland. While the four men waited, Mrs. Johnson went over to a neighbor's house and telephoned Chief Stewart. Meanwhile her husband had convinced Boda that, since the Overland did not have 1920 plates, it would be better to leave it in the garage. Boda apparently took his advice and drove off on the motorcycle with Orciani.

Sacco and Vanzetti left the Johnson house and boarded the North Elm Street trolley for Brockton. When the car was passing through the Campello section of Brockton, it was boarded by a policeman who immediately arrested the two men. The officer found a .38-caliber Harrington & Richardson revolver (which was not Berardelli's) and some shotgun shells in Vanzetti's coat pocket. Sacco denied that he was carrying a gun and "a slight going over" did not reveal any weapon on his person. Later that evening, at the Brockton police station, "an automatic .32 Colt revolver" was found in his belt as well as 32 cartridges of various makes.

Four weeks later, Vanzetti was indicted for an earlier attempted holdup that had taken place at Bridgewater on the morning of December 24, 1919, in which several "foreigners" had tried to hijack a truck containing the payroll of the White Shoe Company. According to eyewitnesses, two men had parked their automobile so that it blocked off Broad Street, the road leading to the shoe company. Guards in the payroll truck had fired at the holdup men who had retreated to their car and driven away. One of the thwarted bandits, who was armed with a shotgun, had discharged his weapon harmlessly at the guards before turning tail.

The trial of this indictment began at Plymouth on June 22, 1920, before Judge Webster Thayer and a jury of 12 men, one of whom was the foreman at the Plymouth Cordage Company from which Vanzetti had been discharged in 1916 for participating in a strike. The charges against the fish peddler were assault with intent to rob and assault with intent to murder. Sacco was not indicted because the records of the 3-K Shoe Factory in Stoughton indicated that he had been at work on the day of the crime.

Frederick G. Katzmann, the district attorney of Suffolk and Plymouth Counties, took the position that the 1920 Buick which had been found in the Manley Woods on April 17, had also been used in the Bridgewater assault. He had three witnesses — the two guards who had been in the payroll truck and a shoe company employee — who identified Vanzetti as the man who had fired the shotgun. A Mrs. Georgina F. Brooks, who had been walking near the Bridgewater railroad station, said that she had seen Vanzetti driving an automobile in the vicinity just after the shooting. Maynard Freeman Shaw, a newsboy, swore that he had seen the defendant that morning running up Broad Street with a gun in his hand. Shaw knew he "was a foreigner, I could tell by the way he ran." Most of the witnesses described the bandits' automobile as a "dark touring car."

The prosecution rested on June 28 and Vanzetti's attorneys, J. P. Vahey and J. M. Graham, put 16 Italians on the stand to prove that the defendant had an alibi for the day of the crime. His landlady said that she had seen Vanzetti preparing his fish on the evening of December 23 and that she had awakened him early the next morning. Other Plymouth residents swore that they had purchased eels from him during the day. John DiCarli bought some shortly after 7:00 a.m. and Mrs. Terese Malaquci an hour later. Between 9:00 a.m. and 10:00 a.m., Beltrando Brini, a 13-year-old boy who worked for Vanzetti, delivered some fish to Mrs. Adeladi Bonjionanni and to her neighbor, Mrs. Margaretta Fiochi. All told, some seven people testified that Vanzetti or the young Brini had filled orders for them on the morning of the 24th. Upon the recommendation of his lawyers, who were afraid that his radical opinions and activities would be brought out, Vanzetti did not take the stand.

The jury retired at 10:50 on the morning of July 1, and returned a verdict of guilty on both assault charges a little more than five hours later. In the middle of August, Judge Thayer sentenced the defendant to 12 to 15 years in prison. As the verdicts were announced, Vanzetti turned to his many friends in the courtroom and said, *"Corragio."* Although a notice of appeal was duly filed with the Supreme Judicial Court, it was never perfected because of the subsequent murder conviction.

On September 11, both Sacco and Vanzetti were indicted for the South Braintree murders by "beating and shooting... against the peace of said Commonwealth." However, it was not until May 31, 1921 that their joint trial began in Dedham, a Boston suburb, before the ubiquitous Judge Thayer. It took more than four days and 700 Norfolk County veniremen before George A. Gerard, the last juror, was sworn in at 1:35 a.m. on June 9. Judge Thayer appointed Walter R. Ripley, a stock-keeper and former Quincy police chief, as foreman and it was at last time for Katzmann to put in his case against the two immigrant defendants.

After Vanzetti's conviction on the assault charges, the Sacco-Vanzetti Defense Committee, headed by Aldino Felicani, editor of *La Notizia,* an Italian-language newspaper, retained Frederick H. Moore and William J. Callahan, for Sacco, and two brothers, Jeremiah J. and Thomas F. McAnarney, for Vanzetti. Moore, a member of the California Bar, was named chief counsel for both men despite strenuous pre-trial efforts by Mrs. Sacco to have him withdraw in favor of William G. Thompson, a Boston attorney. The Commonwealth was again represented by Mr. Katzmann who was aided by Assistant District Attorney Harold P. Williams.

After the physicians who conducted the autopsies on the two murdered men had described their wounds and identified the bullets taken from their bodies, Shelley Neal told the jury about the black sedan he had seen in South Braintree on the day of the crime. He was positive that it was the same car that had been found in the Manley Woods two days later. But, outside of remembering that there had been a slender man with light hair standing next to the Buick when he had seen it parked in front of Hampton House on the morning of the holdup, Neal was unable to describe any of the vehicle's occupants.

Neal wasn't the only prosecution witness who couldn't identify the defendants. Hans Behrsin, Mr. Slater's chauffeur, had observed two "light complexioned fellows" sitting on the fence near Rice & Hutchins just before the shooting. But he was unable to describe them with any certainty because "they were all covered up." After the murders, he had seen the Buick heading for the Pearl Street crossing. When it passed him, "the back curtains were drawn and flopping around back and forth, and I think there were about five of them in there... and as it passed me by there was someone on the back there, beckoning with a gun or shotgun." Because he hadn't got a good look at any of the men in the car, he couldn't say that Sacco or Vanzetti had been riding in it.

Jim Bostock had been taken to see the defendants shortly after their arrest and asked whether they were the men he had seen on Pearl Street that afternoon. Like Behrsin, he "could not tell whether or not they was, no, sir." Lewis Wade could not "say for sure" if Sacco

was the man who had shot Berardelli. Even though he had told
Katzmann at the Brockton police station that the defendant was the
man he had seen, he now thought he had been "a little mite mistak-
en." The reason he was no longer sure of his identification was that
just before the trial he had seen a different man in a barber shop
who resembled the murderer.

Foreman Langlois, who had watched two "young men" firing at
the guard and the paymaster, remembered only that they had been
"short and dark complexioned, curly or wavy hair, about five ft. eight
or nine inches, about 140 or 145 pounds." He was sure that he could
not identify either man if he saw them again. Mark Carrigan had
seen the car race over the crossing but had not been able to recognize anyone in it because it had been going so fast. Louis De
Beradinis, the proprietor of a shoe repair shop at the corner of
Railroad Avenue and Pearl Street, had been frightened by a man
with "a long face... and light hair" who had leaned out of the car and
pointed a gun at him. Although, he thought that dark-haired Sacco
looked like the man with the gun, he insisted that the latter had
been "a light-haired man."

But Katzmann was not wanting for more definite eyewitnesses.
He had five who claimed to have seen Vanzetti near South Braintree
on April 15. John Faulkner said he had observed him, bushy mustache and all, on the Boston train that morning. But he was unable
to remember anything about the man sitting to his immediate right
who had asked him, supposedly at Vanzetti's request, whether the
next station was East Braintree. He admitted that he had seen a picture of the defendant in a newspaper before he was taken to the jail
to identify him. The conductor on the train later testified that he,
too, had seen such a man get off at East Braintree on several occasions long after April 15, but he was certain that he was not Vanzetti.

Harry Dolbeare, the piano tuner, who swore that he had noticed
Vanzetti among a group of "foreigners" sitting in the back of a car
before noon on the day of the shootings, couldn't identify any of the
other men. Although gate tender Levangie was sure that Vanzetti
was the "dark complexioned man" who had frightened him with a
pistol at the Pearl Street crossing, he couldn't remember whether
Mr. McAnarney had visited him at his shanty barely two weeks before
the trial started. Alexander G. Victorson, the railroad's freight clerk,
later testified that Levangie had said, minutes after the shooting, that
he didn't think he could identify the men he had seen in the car as

it sped over the tracks.

An hour later, the gate tender told Henry McCarthy, a locomotive fireman, that he had "ducked in the shanty" when he saw the guns pointed at him. "I asked him if he knew them," McCarthy said, "He said no, he did not. I asked him if he would know them again if he saw them. He said, 'no,' all he could see was the gun and he ducked." Shortly afterward, Levangie informed Timothy J. Collins, a *Boston Globe* reporter, that he had not seen anyone in the car, while at 4:30 p.m., he told Slater & Morrill's Edward Carter that its driver had been "a light-haired man."

Austin T. Reed, the gate tender at the Matfield Crossing in West Bridgewater, identified Vanzetti as the man sitting next to the driver of a "five-passenger car" which had roared toward his intersection at 4:15 p.m. The automobile had screeched to a stop when Reed lowered his gates because of an approaching train. When the train had passed, the car crossed the tracks and pulled up alongside Reed's shanty. Vanzetti, he said, had shouted, "What to hell did you hold us up for?" in "English that was unmistakable and clear." The vehicle then drove off to the east, circled around, and finally recrossed the tracks, disappearing in the direction of West Bridgewater. Like Faulkner, Reed had gone voluntarily to Brockton and "asked to see the two defendants that were there." He had listened to Vanzetti speak to an officer at the police station in "the same gruff tone that he used in speaking to me."

Austin C. Cole was the conductor of the street car on which Sacco and Vanzetti were arrested. He was sure that they were the same two men he had seen on his car on either April 14 or 15. According to him, they had boarded the trolley at Sunset Avenue, some two miles from West Bridgewater's Elm Square. He particularly remembered Vanzetti because he had first thought that the latter was a friend of his named Tony. When the defense showed him a side view photograph of one Joseph Scavitto, a man who bore a striking resemblance to Vanzetti, the witness was unable to say that it was a picture of the man who had boarded his car because he had never seen his profile.

The prosecution had seven witnesses who identified Sacco. Lola Andrews insisted that he was the man she had seen working under the car near Slater & Morrill Factory No. 2. When Katzmann asked her to look around the courtroom, she pointed to the steel cage in which both defendants were seated and said, "That man there." Sacco sprang to his feet and shouted, "I am the man? Do you mean me? Take a good look!" Yes, she was sure that the man who had just yelled at her was the same dark man who had told her how to get to Rice & Hutchins.

Mrs. Andrews claimed that she had picked out Sacco in the Dedham Jail in February. After she had been taken through the prison, she had accidentally seen the defendant in one of the cells. She couldn't remember whether he had been alone or not but she had watched him for at least 15 minutes. No one had told her to look into that particular room. "The room I was in," she said, "was — I don't know just how to explain it, but it had kind of an opening back here, like there was a room underneath, and you could look from the room I was in down into that room."

When Mr. Moore showed her some snapshots and asked her whether she had looked at them before at his request, she stated, "I don't recognize any of those photographs at all." The next day, Mrs. Andrews collapsed on the stand when Mr. McAnarney tried to pin her down as to just what pictures she had seen. Later in the trial, Mrs. Campbell, who had accompanied Mrs. Andrews to South Braintree on April 15, swore that the man under the car had "never looked up at all" and that neither she nor her friend had spoken to him.

But Mrs. Campbell wasn't the only witness to contradict the practical nurse. George W. Fay, a Quincy policeman, said that Mrs. Andrews had told him in February that she had not seen any man's face that day. She had also told Alfred N. LaBreque, the secretary of the Quincy chamber of commerce the same thing. Harry Kurlansky, a tailor whose shop was near Mrs. Andrew's house, remembered a conversation he had had with her when she returned from the Dedham Jail. "The government took me down and want me to recognize those men," she had complained to him, "and I don't know a thing about them. I have never seen them and I can't recognize them." A former landlady, who readily admitted that she didn't like Mrs. Andrews and "wouldn't have her in my house again," also said that she had a "bad name" in the community.

Real estate broker Tracy, who had told the police that he had seen Sacco standing near a Pearl Street drugstore at noon on the day of the murders, had identified him in jail 10 months later. However, he was not prepared now to say that he was "positively" the man. "To the best of my opinion he is the man," he testified. While he was "quite sure" that he was right, he was willing to "suppose the best of people could make a mistake."

Q. Then you feel you could not be mistaken in the identity of
    this man?
A. I said, I would not positively say he was the man; but I wouldn't
    positively say that he wasn't.

William J. Heron, the railroad detective, claimed that he had seen
Sacco handcuffed to a policeman near the Quincy courthouse some
six weeks after having observed him in the South Braintree station.
He was "pretty sure" that the defendant was the same "nervous
Italian" he had watched in the waiting room. He readily admitted
that he had refused to talk to defense investigators when they came
to see him before trial. His reluctance, he said, had been due to the
fact that he didn't want to become involved. Besides, he didn't think
that his information would be helpful to the defense. McAnarney's
face purpled with anger.

Q. You took it on yourself to determine the fact that your evidence
    would hurt these defendants, didn't you? Did you?
A. Yes, sir.

The man whom Lewis Pelser had seen shoot Berardelli had been
wearing a "dark green pair of pants and an army shirt, tucked up."
He would not swear that Sacco was the gunman but insisted that "he
is the dead image of the man I seen." He had written down the
Buick's license number but he had not seen anyone in the car. "I was
too anxious to get away," he said, "I was kind of scared myself."

When Moore took over, he asked the witness whether he had
been interviewed by a Mr. Reid on March 26. Yes, he had, but he
hadn't told him everything he knew because "I didn't know him well
enough." He admitted that he had told the investigator that he had-
n't seen the murderer because he had ducked under his workbench
when the shooting started. But he insisted that he "didn't exactly lie
to Mr. Reid." In fact, he hadn't even told the district attorney what
he had seen that day until he took the stand. Moore's voice was heavy
with disbelief.

Q. You never talked to a living soul and told them what you
    intended to say on the witness stand today, and told them the
    truth, until you got on the witness stand.
A. Yes, sir.

Later, William Brenner, Peter McCullum and Dominic Constantino,

who had been working with Pelser on the first floor of the Rice &
Hutchins factory, testified for the defense that they had not seen the
latter at the window when the shooting took place. According to the
three men, everyone on the first floor had ducked under his bench
when the gunshots had shattered the air. Constantino was sure that
Pelser had not stood up until after the murders had occurred. He
remembered that Pelser had told him that he had not been able to
see any of the killers.

Mary Splaine, the Slater & Morrill bookkeeper, who had picked
Sacco out in the Brockton police station as the man she had seen
leaning out of the Buick just after it roared across the Pearl Street
crossing, identified him again. "He was a man," she claimed, "that I
should say was slightly taller than I am... he was an active-looking
man. I noted particularly the left hand was a good-sized hand, a
hand that denoted strength... He had a gray... what I thought was a
shirt... and the face was what we could call clear-cut, clean-cut face.
The forehead was high. The hair was brushed back and it was
between, I should think, two and two and a half inches in length and
had dark eyebrows, but the complexion was a peculiar white that
looked greenish." Evidently, years of poring over account books had-
n't interfered with the witness's eyesight because this detailed observation had been the result of a three-second glance "from a distance
of 60 to 80 feet."

When Moore reminded her that, at the preliminary examination
at Quincy, she had said that she was not sure that Sacco was the man
she had seen, Miss Splaine denied that she had ever made that
statement. The next day, however, she indicated that perhaps she
had indeed said such a thing.

> Q. Do you wish to change any part of your testimony that you
>   made yesterday?
> A. Yes, sir.
> Q. What part of your testimony would you like to change at the
>   present time?
> A. That question and answer where you asked me if I possibly
>   identified the man. In Quincy I said I didn't feel I would posi-
>   tively identify him. Yesterday I said I didn't say that, but on
>   reflection, that was my answer in Quincy.

In addition, she admitted that, after the shooting, she had identified
in a photograph which the police had shown her, the man she had

observed leaning out of the car. She later learned that the man in the photograph had been in New York's Sing Sing Prison on April 15.

When Mr. McAnarney took over from Moore, he asked the witness whether she was sure that she had had enough time on the day of the murders to get a good look at the defendant. "Yes, sir, I think I did," was her answer. The lawyer shook his head. Hadn't she testified in Quincy that "I don't think my opportunity afforded me the right to say he is the man?" Yes, she had made that statement. But now, she was "positive he is the man, certain he is the man. I admit the possibility of an error, but I am certain I am not making a mistake." McAnarney pressed her.

Q. What did you mean when you said you didn't have sufficient opportunity to observe him?
A. Well, he was passing on the street.
Q. That is the only opportunity you had?
A. Yes, sir.
Q. You have had no other opportunity but that fleeting glance?
A. The remembrance of that.

She hadn't seen Sacco since the Quincy hearing on May 26, 1920, but, even without "any further examination of him," she had changed her mind and now believed that he was the man.

Frances J. Devlin, another Slater & Morrill bookkeeper, who worked in the same room with Miss Splaine, had seen a man in the back of the Buick fire into the crowd that had developed around Parmenter and Berardelli. "He was a dark man," she recalled, "and his forehead, the hair seemed to grow away from the temples, and it was brown-black and he had clear features, rather clear features, and rather good looking, and he had a white complexion and a fairly thick-set man, I should say." She had identified Sacco at the Brockton police station as looking "very much like the man that stood up in the back seat shooting." She was far more definite when Katzmann asked her to look around the courtroom and "see if you see that man." She pointed to the steel cage in which the two defendants were sitting and said, "The man on the inner side as you go out."

Q. The man who is smiling?
A. Yes, sir.
Q. That man you know is Sacco?
A. Yes, sir.

No, there had never been any doubt in her mind "at any time" that the defendant was the man she had seen.

Yet, a year earlier she had testified in Quincy that she couldn't say "positively" whether Sacco was the gunman she had witnessed. But she had a ready answer for the seeming conflict in her testimony. "At the time there I had in my own mind that he was the man, but on account of the immensity of the crime and everything, I hated to say right out and out. I knew he was the man and still I didn't want to say knowing as I knew it would be a deliberate lie, according to my own mind, but still I hated to say right out and out, so I just put it that way." She had also sworn in Quincy that the short, stocky Sacco was "a man who seemed as though he was a big man to me."

Victrola salesman Carlos E. Goodridge was certain that Sacco was the man who had waved a gun at him when the black Buick raced by Magazu's pool parlor on lower Pearl Street. He remembered the defendant as "a dark complexioned fellow with dark hair and he had... a kind of peculiar face, that came down pointed." When McAnarney tried to find out whether Goodridge wasn't having his own problems with the law, Judge Thayer intervened. "You can't attack any witness's credibility," he observed, "except by showing a record of conviction." The jury was never to learn that the salesman had recently pleaded guilty to larceny and had been placed on probation.

Goodridge's testimony conflicted sharply with that of Harry Arrogani, a South Braintree barber. Five or six days after the murders, Goodridge had told the barber that he had seen "a man in the car but if I have got to say who the man was, I can't say." Peter Magazu, the owner of the pool room, said that Goodridge had described the man who had pointed the gun at him as a "young man with light hair, light complexion." Andrew Manganio, Goodridge's sales manager, later testified that his pool-playing employee had refused to identify the defendants in jail because he had been so frightened by the gun that "he could not possibly remember the faces."

Drs. George B. Magrath and Nathaniel S. Hunting had conducted the autopsies on the two murdered men. Four bullets were found in Berardelli's body and two in Parmenter's. As each bullet was removed, the physicians had scratched a Roman numeral in its base. The one which had caused Berardelli's death, a .32-caliber Winchester, was marked No. III. At the trial, Captain William H.

Proctor, the ballistics expert for the Massachusetts State Police, testified that all but the No. III shell had been fired through a Savage automatic pistol.

When Sacco was searched at the Brockton police station, a ".32 Colt automatic," which was to become Katzmann's Exhibit 28, was found in his belt. Proctor said that he had conducted tests on the fatal bullet and the defendant's gun. As a result of his investigation, he was prepared to say that No. III was "consistent with being fired by that pistol." As for the other five bullets, his opinion was that they had not been fired from Sacco's Colt.

Captain Proctor's opinion was shared by Charles Van Amburgh, an assistant in the ballistics department of the Remington Arms Company. He also had examined the fatal bullet and Sacco's pistol.

> Q. Have you formed an opinion... as to whether or not the No.
> III bullet was fired from that particular Colt automatic?
> A. I have an opinion.
> Q. And what is your opinion?
> A. I am inclined to believe that it was fired, the No. III bullet was
> fired, from this Colt automatic pistol.

He had reached this conclusion after comparing the No. III bullet with six test shots which he and Captain Proctor had fired into oiled sawdust at Lowell, Massachusetts. "My measurement of rifling marks on the No. III bullet as compared with the width of the impressions which I have taken of the No. III and of this particular barrel," he explained, "together with the measurements of the width or dimension of rifling marks in bullets recovered... in Lowell, inclines me to the belief." In addition, he had observed marks on No. III which he thought were caused by pitting in the groove of Sacco's Colt.

James E. Burns, an expert marksman who had been employed by the U.S. Cartridge Company for more than 30 years, contradicted the prosecution's experts. He, too, had examined the fatal bullet, and he was convinced that it had not been fired from Sacco's gun.

> Q. ...on what do you base that opinion?
> A. On the 11 bullets that I examined that were fired from the
> Sacco gun. It doesn't compare with them at all.

The Colt's barrel had shown "a clean-cut lead all the way through." There wasn't a particle of doubt in Burns's mind that No. III had not been fired "from a gun that had a clean lead."

J. Henry Fitzgerald, the director of the testing room at the Colt Firearms Company, agreed with Burns that No. III "was not fired from the pistol given to me as Exhibit 28." He had examined three bullets which had been fired by Mr. Van Amburgh at Lowell, and "the land marks of the No. III bullet do not correspond, in my best judgment, to bullets I have seen fired from this pistol." Like Burns, he had been unable to find any distinctive pittings in the groove of Sacco's gun.

The cap which Fred L. Loring had found lying near Berardelli's body had been turned over to Thomas F. Fraher, Slater & Morrill's superintendent. Katzmann called George T. Kelley, Sacco's foreman at the 3-K Shoe Factory, who testified that the defendant often wore a cap to work. "There were times that he wore a cap," Kelley said, "There was other times he wore a hat." As to the former, he could remember only that it had been "a dark cap... of a salt and pepper design." He was unable to recall whether the cap he had seen hanging on a nail near Sacco's workbench had earlaps or not.

When the defense objected to the introduction of the cap on the ground that it had not been sufficiently identified as belonging to Sacco, Judge Thayer ordered Mr. Williams to ask Kelley whether "that cap... is like the one that was worn by the defendant Sacco?" "In color only," the witness replied.

> Thayer: That is not responsive to the question. I wish you would answer it, if you can.
> Kelley: I can't answer it when I don't know right down in my heart if that is the cap.
> Thayer: In its general appearance, is it the same?
> Kelley: Yes, sir.

Thayer promptly admitted the cap into evidence as the Commonwealth's Exhibit 29.

After Sacco's arrest, Lieutenant Daniel T. Guerin had visited his home and found another cap in the kitchen. Later in the trial, when Kelley was recalled as a witness for the defense, he was shown this second cap. He said he thought that the cap the policeman had found, looked more like the one he had seen the defendant wearing than did Exhibit 29. On cross-examination, Katzmann asked Kelley if he hadn't told the police, when they interviewed him about the cap, "I have an opinion... but I don't want to get a bomb up my ass." Kelley admitted that he "might have said it when they drove off, but not at the time when they showed me the cap."

> Q. Was that in reference to the cap?
> A. Yes.

Later in the trial, when Katzmann cross-examined Sacco, he asked him to put Exhibit 29 on his head. According to the *Boston Herald*, "It stuck on the top of his head and he turned with a satisfied air to let the jury see." He then explained to the district attorney that the cap was "too tight" to fit properly.

> Q. You are sure of that?
> A. I am pretty sure. I can feel it.

He denied that the cap was his and his wife subsequently testified that her husband "never wore caps with anything around for his ears, never, because he never liked it and because, besides that, never, he never wore them because he don't look good in them, positively."

Mrs. Simon Johnson said that, after her husband had gone to bed on May 5, Boda had knocked on her front door and asked her whether he could pick up his Overland car. When she awakened her husband, he had told her to go next door to Mrs. Bartlett's and telephone the police. She had walked over to her neighbor's house and called Chief Stewart. Although there was no street lights near her home, the area had been illuminated by the headlight of a motorcycle which she noticed was parked in the street. Two strange men who were standing in the vicinity of the vehicle, seemed to follow her when she left to make her call. Ten minutes later, when she was walking back from Mrs. Bartlett's, she saw the same men who appeared to be "walking along" with her. She was sure that Sacco was one of the men who had tailed her that night.

When she had testified in the earlier trial of Vanzetti at Plymouth, Mrs. Johnson had not been so confident of her identification of the men who had followed her. Then, in fact, she had been certain that she "did not know who they were or whether they were the same men or not." Now, she was prepared to say that "one of them" was the same man.

> Q. ...do you want to say that you recognized Sacco before you went into the Bartlett house?
> A. I would know him if I saw him again.
> Q. I submit it is not an answer to the question.

THE COURT. Can you answer it, Mrs. Johnson, by Yes or No?
A. Yes.
Q. Then by that I assume you mean you did recognize him before
   you went into the Bartlett house?
A. Before I did, yes.

The witness's husband told a somewhat different story. At no time
had either of the strange men been illuminated by the beams of the
motorcycle's light. While he had not watched his wife walk over to
the Bartlett's, he had seen her on the return trip. At that time, he was
sure that, with the exception of Boda, all the strangers were standing
near the cycle. He had told Boda that he couldn't have the car that
night because "there were no 1920 number plates on it." The latter
had replied, "I will send somebody for it tomorrow," but no one had
ever called for the car.

Michael J. Connolly and Earl J. Vaughan, two Brockton policemen, had arrested the defendants on the North Elm Street trolley
later that evening. Connolly was the first officer to board the car. "I
went down through the car," he said, "and when I got opposite the
seat I stopped and I asked them where they came from. They said,
'We went down to see a friend of mine.' I said, 'Who is your friend?'
He said 'A man by the name of — they call him 'Poppy.' 'Well,' I
said, 'I want you, you are under arrest.' "

According to Connolly, Vanzetti, who had been sitting on the
seat nearest the window, put his hand in his hip pocket. The policeman had shouted, "Keep your hands out on your lap, or you will be
sorry!" When the two defendants asked him why they were being
arrested, he had told them that they were "suspicious characters."
Vaughan then boarded the car and Connolly ordered Vanzetti to
stand up so that the latter could "fish" him. He himself gave Sacco "a
slight going over... did not go into his pockets."

Q. Was anything found on either man at that time?
A. There was a revolver found on Vanzetti.

The two suspects were then transferred to a police car which was
waiting alongside the tracks. Connolly "put Sacco and Vanzetti in the
back seat... and Officer Snow got in the back seat with them. I took
the front seat with the driver, facing Sacco and Vanzetti." During the
trip to the Brockton station house, Connolly noticed that Sacco
"reached his hand to put under his overcoat and I told him to keep

his hands outside of his clothes and on his lap." When he asked the defendant, "Have you got a gun there?" the latter had replied, "No, I ain't got no gun." Merle A. Spear, the driver of the car, swore that he had heard this conversation and that Sacco had answered, "You need not be afraid of me." Later that evening, a Colt revolver had been found in Sacco's pocket.

Chief Stewart had arrived at the police station shortly after 11:00 that night. The two prisoners told him much the same story that they had related to Connolly. They insisted that they had gone to West Bridgewater to see a friend named Poppy but denied any knowledge of Boda or Orciani's motorcycle. Sacco thought that they had left his house at 6:30 p.m. that day while Vanzetti was sure that they had started out three hours earlier. Sacco claimed that he had purchased his Colt in Hanover Street in Boston many months before his arrest.

On June 22, after 59 witnesses had testified for the prosecution, Katzmann informed Judge Thayer that "We believe we have nothing further to offer... the Commonwealth rests, if your Honor please." Following Callahan's opening statement, the defense promptly called Frank J. Burke, the glassblower who had watched the Buick race over the Pearl Street crossing after the murders. He had gotten a good look at its passengers and he was certain that neither defendant had been in the car. "I would say they were not," he said. But on cross-examination, Katzmann succeeded in showing that the witness had such poor eyes that he had thought that Mr. Callahan's Hudson in which he had been driven to the courthouse that very morning was a Buick.

Mrs. Barbara Liscomb, the Rice & Hutchins employee who had fainted when one of the gunmen pointed his pistol at her, "would always remember his face." When she had been taken to the Brockton police station, she had been unable to identify either defendant.

> Q. And you have looked at these men in the dock?
> A. I have.
> Q. Are either of the men in the dock the man you saw pointing the revolver at your window?
> A. No, sir.

She was "positively sure" that she had never seen either Sacco or Vanzetti before.

Jennie Novelli, a nurse, who, some 10 minutes before the shooting, had seen the Buick proceeding slowly up Pearl Street in the direction of the Rice & Hutchins plant, said the man who had been sitting next to the driver was not Sacco although she had previously told a detective that a photograph of the defendant "resembled" the man she had seen in the car. Albert Frantello insisted that the defendants were not the men he had noticed leaning against the Rice & Hutchins fence before the murders. None of the laborers at the restaurant excavation or the railroad employees who had been repairing tracks at the Pearl Street crossing could say that they had seen Sacco or Vanzetti in the vicinity of the crime. In all, some two dozen eyewitnesses testified that they had not seen either defendant in South Braintree on April 15, 1920.

Vanzetti was the first of the two defendants to take the stand. As far as the day of the murder was concerned, he insisted, in broken English, that he had not left Plymouth. In the morning, he had been "selling fish from a cart" on Castle and Cherry Streets. Some time during the morning, he had asked Joseph Rosen, a peddler, to accompany him to the home of Mrs. Alphonsine Brini so that she could look at a piece of cloth which Rosen wanted to sell to him. Vanzetti thought that this had taken place "near 1:00 p.m., about half past 11, something like that, half past 12, about one o'clock."

After he had sold all his fish, the defendant had visited Melvin Corl, a friend of his, who was painting his boat. He had had a long conversation with Corl — about an hour and a half — during which time he had also talked to a boat builder by the name of Frank Jesse. Then he had gone home, changed his clothes, and eaten his supper. He could not remember what he had done after finishing his dinner.

On May 5, he had accompanied Boda to the Johnson home in order to pick up the latter's car which was to be used in collecting radical literature from the homes of some of his friends "in five or six places, five or six towns." The mysterious death in New York, on May 3, of Andrea Salsedo, a radical with whom he had been associated for many years, had convinced him that he should "get the books and literature to put at some place and hide not to find by the police or the state." He had not told the police about his plans for that night "because in that time, there was the deportation and the reaction was more vivid than now and more mad than now."

He readily admitted that he had lied to Stewart when the police chief had questioned him after his arrest. "I was afraid," he said, "he went into the house of the people that they named and found some literature or paper and arrested the men... I was scared to give the names and addresses of my friends as I knew that almost all of them have some books and some newspapers in their house by which the authorities take a reason for arresting them and deporting them." His fears had been aggravated by the fact that officers Connolly and Vaughan had refused to tell him why he was being taken into custody.

> Q. What did they say you were arrested for?
> A. They say, "Oh, you know, you know why." And when I try to sleep in the cell, there is no blanket, only the wood. Then we called for the blanket, because it was rather cool. They say, "Never mind, you catch warm by and by, and tomorrow morning we put you in a line in the hall between the chairs and we shoot you."

In fact, during the night, one of his jailers had spit in his face and threatened him with a revolver.

Vanzetti also conceded that he had lied to Katzmann when the district attorney had questioned him about the price he had paid for his revolver, the number of times he had visited Boston overnight, and his acquaintance with Boda. Again he based his reluctance to tell the truth on his desire to shield his friends. "I intend to not mention the name and house of my friends" he explained.

Joseph Rosen testified that he had sold Vanzetti several pieces of cloth at noon on April 15. Mrs. Brini remembered that she had seen the defendant selling fish that morning and that he and Rosen had come to her house to get her opinion as to the worth of some swatches of material. Her daughter, LeFavre, had also seen the fish peddler on both occasions. At noon, Angel T. Guidobone, a rug worker, had purchased some codfish from Vanzetti. Melvin Corl recalled that the defendant had visited him when he was painting his boat, and Frank Jesse stated that he had talked to Vanzetti about an automobile while they were watching Corl at work.

Sacco confirmed Vanzetti's testimony that both men had told falsehoods because they were afraid that they had been arrested for their radical activities. Since the police had not informed them of the nature of the charges against them, he had been convinced that he and Vanzetti had been picked up because they had been working "for the movement, for the working class, for the laboring class." In fact, one of the first things Officer Stewart had asked Sacco was whether he was a socialist.

Q. When he asked you what you were in Bridgewater for, did you
    give him a true reason for being there?
A. No, sir, because I was afraid to arrest us, they arrest somebody
    else of the people...

Like Vanzetti, he freely admitted that he was a socialist who did not
believe in war. After the United States entered the war in 1917, both
he and his codefendant had run away to Mexico to avoid the draft.
Sacco had returned to Massachusetts several months later under an
alias and had not resumed his real name until after the war ended. As
he put it, "What right do we have to kill each other? I don't believe in
no war. I want to destroy those guns." He loved his adopted country,
but his hatred of war was greater than his devotion to an abstraction.

As far as April 15 was concerned, he maintained that he had
spent the entire day in Boston. In the middle of March, he had
received a letter informing him that his mother had died in Italy. He
had decided to take his family back to the old country and had gone
to Boston on the day of the murders to have his passport validated at
the Italian Consulate. He had taken the 8:56 a.m. train from
Stoughton and, after arriving at South Station, had walked to
Hanover Street where he had met Angelo Monello, a Roxbury con-
tractor. Then he had gone to Boni's Restaurant for lunch with Felice
Guadagni, the editor of an Italian journal. The two men were later
joined by John D. Williams, a space salesman for several foreign-lan-
guage newspapers, and Albert Bosco, a *La Notizia* editor.

He loved his adopted country, but his hatred of war was greater than his devotion to an abstraction.

Sacco had left Boni's at 1:30 p.m. and gone to the consulate. He
was told by some man there that the photograph he had brought was
much too big to fit on a passport. Then he had dropped in at a nearby coffee house where he had again met Guadagni and Antonio
Dentamore, a former newspaperman. At 3:20 p.m., after buying
some groceries at a nearby store, he had paid a debt of $15 to a man
named Affe. Then, he had caught the 4:12 p.m. train back to
Stoughton, arriving home shortly after 6:00 p.m. Katzmann was
remorseless in his cross-examination. Why hadn't the defendant
gone to the consulate in the morning and taken the noon train back

to Stoughton? "Well, I think to pass all day when I been in Boston," was the reply. Hadn't he lied to George Kelley, his foreman, when he had told him that there was such a crowd in there you could not get your passport and the place closed and you missed the noon train for that reason? Yes, he had lied to Mr. Kelley. He also hadn't told the truth at Brockton when he claimed that he had worked on the 15th. "I was not sure," he explained, "There was not interest to me very close to find out the date I have been out."

A bevy of witnesses paraded to the stand to buttress Sacco's alibi. Dominick Ricci said that he had seen the shoemaker early on the morning of the 15th at the Stoughton railroad station. At 11:00 a.m., Angelo Monello had passed the time of day with him in East Boston. Guadagni, Williams and Bosco verified the lunch at Boni's. According to an affidavit submitted by Guiseppe Andrower, the former passport officer at the Italian consulate, Sacco had come to his window at 2:00 p.m. and shown him a photograph which the official had said was too large for a passport. "April 15, 1920, was a very quiet day," he swore, "and since such a large photograph had never been before presented for use on a passport, I took it in and showed it to the secretary of the consulate. We laughed and talked over the incident."

At 2:45 p.m., at Giordani's coffee house, the defendant had complained to Dentamore that he would have to go to the expense of having another picture taken for his passport. Carlos M. Affe remembered that Sacco had dropped in at his grocery store between 3:00 p.m. and 4:00 p.m. to pay an outstanding bill of $15.50. Mrs. Sacco, who testified through an interpreter, knew that her husband had gone to Boston on the 15th because that was the day she had been visited by Henry Iacovelli, a friend from Milford. Mr. Iacovelli confirmed that he had indeed called at the Sacco home that day.

As for their guns, each defendant had an explanation. Vanzetti claimed that he had bought his for $5 from a friend named Luigi Falzini in early 1920 because "it was a very bad time and I like to have a revolver for self defense."

> Q. What do you mean, "It was a bad time?"
> A. Bad time, I mean it was many crimes, many holdups, many robberies.

Sacco maintained that he had been in the habit of carrying a gun when he had worked as a night watchman at the 3-K Shoe Factory.

On the day he was arrested, he and Vanzetti had planned "to go to shoot in the woods" but had not done so because "we started an argument and I forgot..."

On July 14, after Judge Thayer had delivered his charge from a flower-bedecked bench, the jury retired. Some seven hours later, it filed back into the courtroom. When Clerk Worthington asked if it had reached a verdict, Foreman Walter R. Ripley announced that it had. He and his colleagues had found each defendant guilty of murder in the first degree. Thayer was happy to express the Commonwealth's gratitude for "the service that you have rendered. You may now go to your homes, from which you have been absent for nearly seven weeks." As the 12 men hurried to take his Honor's welcome advice, Sacco shouted, "They kill an innocent man! They kill two innocent men!"

His prophecy was somewhat premature. On November 5, a motion for a new trial on the ground that the verdict was against the weight of evidence was argued before Thayer. On the day before Christmas, it was denied. As far as the judge was concerned, he would not "announce to the world that these 12 jurors violated the sanctity of their oaths, threw to the four winds of bias and prejudice their honor, judgment, reason and conscience, and thereby abused the solemn trust reposed in them by the law as well as the court." If any errors had been committed during the trial, no one would be happier than he if the Supreme Judicial Court corrected them. "But until that time comes," he said, "so far as these motions are concerned, the verdicts of the jury must stand."

Before Thayer's decision, Jeremiah McAnarney had learned that, during the trial, Foreman Ripley had exhibited some .38 caliber cartridges to other members of the jury. Unfortunately, Ripley died before the lawyer could obtain a statement from him. However, two of his fellow jurors admitted that they had seen the bullets and, on the strength of this, the defense attorneys filed the first of six supplementary motions for a new trial. In their briefs, they argued that it was improper for the jurors to have considered any but legitimate exhibits.

To buttress their position that Ripley was hopelessly prejudiced against the defendants, their lawyers submitted an affidavit by William H. Daly, a good friend of the ex-foreman, who stated that he had run into him at a railroad station several days before the trial. When Daly had expressed some doubt as to whether Sacco and

Vanzetti were guilty, Ripley had replied, "Damn them, they ought to hang them anyway." The prosecution offered no evidence to contradict the Daly affidavit.

In early October of 1921, Frank J. Burke, the glassblower who had testified for the defense, ran into Roy E. Gould in Portland, Maine. The razor paste peddler had never been called as a witness despite the fact that he had given his name to the police. When the black Buick had driven by him, he had gotten a good look at its occupants. According to his sworn statement, which Moore used as the basis of his second supplementary motion, "the man that he saw at South Braintree on April 15, 1920, at or about the hour of 3:00 in the afternoon, riding in the bandit car, front seat, on the right-hand side of the driver, is not the man that he saw in the Dedham County Jail, and who was pointed out to him as Nicola Sacco." As far as Vanzetti was concerned, Gould had seen photographs of the condemned man and "he in no sense resembles the man I saw at South Braintree on April 15, 1920."

On February 4, 1922, Lewis Pelser admitted to Moore, in writing, that he had perjured himself at the trial. His original statement to a defense investigator that he hadn't seen anyone in the bandits' car because he had been huddling under his workbench was, he now admitted, the true story. Pelser's retraction was made part of the Gould motion. However, several days later, he wrote a letter to Katzmann in which he claimed that he had been drinking "pretty heavy" when Moore interviewed him. "He asked me one question and another," he wrote, "and finally my whole story contradicted what I had said at the Dedham court." He had decided to write to the district attorney because he was "worried at the way they have framed me up and got me into trouble."

Moore's third motion was based on the fact that Carlos Goodridge, the Victrola salesman who had rushed out of Magazu's poolroom just as the Buick drove by, had not used his right name at the trial. Furthermore, the lawyer alleged that Goodridge had twice been convicted of theft in New York and that, when he testified, he was a fugitive from a third indictment. In opposing Moore's motion, Katzmann introduced an affidavit from the salesman, admitting most of the defense's contentions, but insisting that his testimony had been accurate.

On September 11, 1922, Moore filed a fourth motion. Two days earlier, Lola Andrews had signed an affidavit in which she repudiated the testimony she had given at Dedham, claiming that she had been coerced by the district attorney and the police. Now she was prepared to state that "each and every part of her testimony... wherein she identified the said Nicola Sacco as the person that she had seen on April 15, 1920, is false and untrue." To the best of her knowledge, she had never seen the defendant until he was pointed out to her in the Dedham County Jail.

Four months later, Mrs. Andrews retracted this repudiation. She told Katzmann that Moore and his associates had threatened to prosecute her and her son if she did not sign a statement which indicated "that I had told a lie, that I did not at any time see Sacco at South Braintree." She would never have signed the paper if her son hadn't put his arm around her and said, "Mother, sign this paper and have an end to all this trouble, for you did not recognize these men, and you will be doing a terrible wrong if you send those men to the chair." She now maintained that she had told the truth at Dedham.

In April of 1923, Albert H. Hamilton, a well-known criminologist, who had testified in more than 165 murder trials, examined all the exhibits in the case. He came to the conclusion that the fatal bullet had not been fired from Sacco's gun. He was supported in his thesis by a member of the faculty of the Massachusetts Institute of Technology. In opposing this motion — the defense's fifth — Katzmann submitted affidavits by several arms experts, disputing Hamilton's claims.

As an adjunct to the Hamilton motion, William G. Thompson, who had come into the case in 1923, filed an affidavit by William H. Proctor. Captain Proctor, who had testified for the Commonwealth that the No. III bullet was "consistent with having been fired" from Sacco's pistol, now explained that he had meant to say only that it was "fired from a Colt automatic pistol of .32-caliber." He insisted that he had "repeatedly" told Katzmann that he could not swear that the "so-called mortal bullet... passed through Sacco's pistol."

"Had I been asked the direct question," he stated, "whether I had found any affirmative evidence whatsoever that this... bullet had passed through Sacco's particular pistol, I should have answered then, as I do now without hesitation, in the negative."

After hearing argument on all these motions, Thayer denied each one, on October 1, 1924. He did not feel that the "mere production" of Ripley's cartridges in the jury room had in any way prejudiced the defendants and, besides, he was unwilling to "blacken the memory" of the dead juror. As far as Gould was concerned, he was convinced that the razor paste salesman must have been mistaken. He disposed of the Pelser retraction by blaming it on an excess of liquor. The motion attacking Goodridge's veracity because of a previous criminal record was a "bold and cruel attempt to sandbag Goodridge by threatening actual arrest" which he could only attribute to Mr. Moore's "overenthusiastic interest in his client's cause." Lastly, Mrs. Andrews' repudiation had been procured by duress, Hamilton's opinion was unconvincing, and, if Captain Proctor had really believed that the fatal bullet did not come from Sacco's gun, he had had ample opportunity at the trial to make himself clear.

After Judge Thayer's decision, all of the defense attorneys except Thompson withdrew from the case. On May 12, 1926, the five-judge Supreme Judicial Court of Massachusetts, in a 60-page opinion, affirmed the trial judge's denial of the various motions. Two weeks later, Thompson filed another application for a new trial, this time based on the admission by one Celestino F. Medeiros, a convicted murderer, who had sent a note to Sacco in jail, in which he confessed that he had participated "in the South Braintree shoe company crime, and Sacco and Vanzetti was not involved in said crime."

Although Medeiros would not name the men who had been associated with him in the Slater & Morrill holdup, he was willing to reveal every other aspect of the crime. He had met the four other members of the gang in a Providence saloon and they had driven to Randolph in a Hudson which they exchanged for a Buick in some woods outside of town. Then they proceeded to South Braintree, killed Parmenter and Berardelli, and drove back to the woods where they abandoned the Buick and raced back to Providence in the Hudson. Medeiros's role during the holdup was to sit in the rear of the Buick with a gun and "help hold back the crowd in case they made a rush."

Despite all of Thompson's astuteness, Medeiros would not name any names. The most the lawyer could get from him was the fact that the gang had been composed of Italians who "had been engaged in robbing freight cars in Providence." At the time of the South Braintree murders, a group of criminals known as the Morelli gang had been hijacking freight cars throughout New England. In fact, on April 15, 1920, several of its members were out on bail awaiting trial for stealing shoes which had been consigned by both Slater & Morrill and Rice & Hutchins. Medeiros' descriptions of his confederates fitted the known members of the Morelli group.

Although Felix Frankfurter was convinced that Medeiros, who maintained that he had confessed because "I seen Sacco's wife come up here with the kids and I felt sorry for the kids," was telling the truth, Judge Thayer felt otherwise. As far as he was concerned, Medeiros was unworthy of belief because he was "a crook, a thief, a robber, a liar, a rum-runner, a 'bouncer' in a house of ill-fame, a smuggler, and a man who has been convicted and sentenced to death for... murder." If Medeiros was so eager to save two men whom he claimed were innocent, why didn't he reveal the names of the other men who had supposedly participated in the Slater & Morrill caper? Furthermore, he felt that Medeiros's haziness as to certain details of the crime clearly indicated that he had not been there.

On April 5, 1927, Thayer's denial was affirmed by the appellate court. Four days later, the two defendants were brought before Thayer for sentencing. After both men had made statements affirming their innocence, Thayer ordered that they "suffer the punishment of death by the passage of a current of electricity through your body within the week beginning on Sunday, the 10th day of July, in the year of our Lord, one thousand, nine hundred and twenty-seven." As the judge was intoning the death sentence, Sacco interrupted to shout, "You know I am innocent. That is the same words I pronounced seven years ago. You condemn two innocent men."

On May 3, Vanzetti wrote to Governor Alvan T. Fuller, on behalf of Sacco and himself, requesting clemency. Fuller's response was to appoint an advisory committee composed of President Abbott Lawrence Lowell of Harvard, President Samuel W. Stratton of MIT and Probate Judge Robert Grant, to investigate the evidence against the condemned men. Because the three-week hearing didn't begin until July 1, the executions were postponed for one month. On July 27, the committee's members reported to the governor that they had "seen no evidence sufficient to make them believe that the trial was unfair." One week later, Fuller stated that he had found "no sufficient justification for executive intervention."

"I believe, with the jury," he said, "that these men, Sacco and Vanzetti, were guilty and that they had a fair trial."

Since the executions were scheduled for August 10, a variety of petitions and motions were filed with everyone from Judge Thayer to Mr. Justice Oliver Wendell Holmes, all without success. In order to give the defense time to appeal several of these denials to the Supreme Judicial Court, Fuller granted a reprieve until August 22. Two days earlier, petitions for certiorari were filed with the clerk of the U.S. Supreme Court but Justices Holmes, Brandeis, Stone and Taft refused to halt the executions. As Holmes put it, "I cannot say that I have a doubt and therefore I must deny the stay."

At 12:19 on the morning of August 23, 1927, Sacco died in the electric chair at Charlestown State Prison. Seven minutes later, he was joined in death by his friend Vanzetti who wished "to forgive some people for what they are doing to me." Perhaps the several thousand people who milled around the prison that torrid August night could take some small measure of comfort from Vanzetti's remarks to a newspaper reporter on the seventh anniversary of the South Braintree shooting: "If it had not been for these things, I might have lived out my life, talking at street corners to scorning men. I might have died, unmarked, unknown, a failure. Now, we are not a failure. This is our career and our triumph. Never in our full life can we hope to do such work for tolerance, for justice, for man's understanding of man, as now we do by an accident. Our words, our lives, our plans — nothing! The taking of our lives, lives of a good shoemaker and a poor fish peddler — all. That last moment belongs to us. That agony is our triumph."

"Our words, our lives, our plans — nothing! The taking of our lives, lives of a good shoemaker and a poor fish peddler — all. That last moment belongs to us. That agony is our triumph."

–Bartolomeo Vanzetti

Scopes – The "Monkey Trial"

Tennessee v. John Thomas Scopes

When George W. Bush was running for office, he said: "On the issue of evolution, the verdict is still out on how God created the Earth." It is also well known that the attorney general of the United States, John Ashcroft, is a born-again Christian who takes daily Bible study classes at the Justice Department.

Most people probably do not know that the first trial of John Thomas Scopes in 1925, for teaching evolution to schoolchildren, ended in his conviction. Tennessee enacted legislation, as had 15 other states, making it a crime to "teach any theory that denies the story of divine creation as taught by the Bible and to teach instead that man was descended from a lower order of animals." Scopes acknowledged that he had taught evolution and, at the end of the trial, his lawyer, the famous Clarence Darrow, asked the judge to instruct the jury to find a guilty verdict so that the case could be appealed to higher court. Scopes was fined $100.

Darrow never believed that Scopes would be acquitted before the case reached the Supreme Court. What Darrow desired was a decision by the U.S. Supreme Court finding that the banning of the teaching of evolution violated the First Amendment to the U.S. Constitution. That amendment prohibits the government, whether state or federal, from passing laws that favor a particular religion or religious belief. In this case, Tennessee state law clearly did so, forbidding the teaching of a scientifically based theory that conflicted with a biblical, Christian belief in divine creation. Despite this, the Scopes case never achieved the legal ruling desired by Scopes and his lawyers. The highest court in Tennessee upheld the statute, but reversed Scopes's conviction on technical grounds.

However, as Bill Kunstler points out, the trial did make a mockery of the theory of divine creation. The defense's examination of William Jennings Bryan, the lawyer for the state of Tennessee, made a laughing stock out of Bryan and stripped any legitimacy from creationism. No one has since been prosecuted in Tennessee for teaching evolution.

The goal of declaring such laws unconstitutional was not achieved until 1968 in the case of *Epperson v. Arkansas*, where the Supreme Court ruled the law unconstitutional because of the prohibition on favoring a particular religion or religious belief over another. Many thought, or at least hoped, that the Supreme Court decision would have put an end to the efforts of religious zealots to impose their creationist views on others. This, however, has not been the case. In the early 1980s, laws were passed in some states that required the teaching of both evolution and creationism. These laws as well were held to be unconstitutional. Then, in 1999, a conservative Christian-dominated school board in Kansas voted to stop requiring that students be tested on their understanding of evolution. This would mean, inevitably, that many teachers would not teach the subject (teachers wanting to teach and students wanting to learn only those subjects that are required to pass state education tests). The Kansas law was widely ridiculed and in 2000 a new school board was elected and the law was overturned.

The latest twist on creationism is called "Intelligent Design" and is being employed by creationists with the hope that they can avoid the constitutional problems of earlier efforts to bring the Bible into the classroom. Intelligent Design is the belief that, given the complexity and diversity of life, an "intelligent designer" must be at work. Its proponents accept that changes can happen within a species, but believe that the intervention of God or an outside force is necessary for one species to evolve into another.

It is difficult to believe that this new twist is taken seriously, being nothing but old wine in new bottles. But we are in a time of religious fervor in the United States and some of our key elected officials might well support the teaching of Intelligent Design. This is perhaps the reason Intelligent Design is being taken more seriously then it deserves. Today, a number of states are considering requiring the teaching of that belief. In 2001, the state of Ohio was drafting new learning standards for students and a committee of scientists and parents reaffirmed the central place of evolution in teaching biology. When the standards went to the state school board, several members wanted them rewritten, that evolution was an "assumption" and they wanted Intelligent Design taught as an alternative. In March 2002, the school board staged a debate between evolutionists and advocates of Intelligent Design giving each the same amount of time to argue their positions. Almost one-third of the school board wanted Ohio students to learn about Intelligent Design. As of this writing, the school board has made no decision.

All of this is to say that the issues presented in the Scopes trial are still with us today. On a superficial level, the case concerns the legitimacy of the teaching of evolution. More deeply, *Scopes v. Tennessee* is about whether or not a belief in the Bible and God can be imposed by the state on its citizens. We might believe we have come a long way since Scopes's trial. This new effort to bring God back into the classroom is a warning that we must remain ever vigilant and not rest upon past victories. That is true especially now with the Bush-Ashcroft religious right occupying the halls of power.

Michael Ratner

Macon County was, in 1925, one of Tennessee's most rural areas. Without a single mile of railroad track, its almost unbroken stretches of farmland were tilled by a God-fearing, Bible-reading population whose sole contact with the outside world consisted of weekly visits to LaFayette, the tiny county seat. Its representative in the lower house of the state legislature was one John Washington Butler, a combination farmer-school teacher, who worked 120 acres just outside of LaFayette.

Butler had first run for election in 1922 on a platform that stressed the need for a law prohibiting the teaching of evolution in the public schools of Tennessee. During his first term, he was evidently much too engrossed with finding his way around Nashville to do any legislating, but he assured his constituents that, if they sent him back for a second stint, he would find the time to push an antievolution bill. The good people of Macon County believed him and, in November 1924, he was resoundingly reelected to the House of Representatives.

When he returned to the capital the following January, he lost no time in living up to his campaign promise. He drafted a statute that would make it unlawful for any public school teacher "to teach any theory that denies the story of the divine creation of man as taught in the Bible, and to teach instead that man has descended from a lower order of animals." The penalty was a fine ranging between $100 and $500. Butler threw his bill into the legislative hopper, saw that it reached the floor of the house, and then promptly washed his hands of it.

By all odds, the proposed legislation should have died a-borning. But with surprisingly strong Baptist support, it carried the lower house on January 28, 1925 by a vote of 71 to five. The next day, Williams Jennings Bryan, who had been fighting Darwinism up and down rural United States, roared into Nashville with his rhetorical, "Is the Bible True?" harangue. Every word of it was, he assured his enthusiastic audience, some of whom were so carried away by his oratory that they printed his speech and sent it to each member of the legislature. Six weeks later, the Butler Act skipped handily through the Senate by a vote of 24 to six. On March 21, a skeptical Governor Austin Peay signed it into law because he was convinced that it would never be "an active statute." He couldn't have been more mistaken.

Up in New York, Roger Baldwin, the director of the struggling American Civil Liberties Union (ACLU), read a report of the new statute in a Tennessee newspaper. He sent a press release to the Memphis, Chattanooga and Knoxville papers, announcing that the ACLU would gladly finance a test case against the Butler Act if only it could find a Tennessee teacher with enough gumption to violate the law. A month later, a mining engineer named George W. Rappelyea, who managed the Dayton mines of the Cumberland Coal and Iron Company, informed Baldwin that he was in a position to arrange a test case. His offer was promptly accepted.

Rappelyea, who had been raised on New York's Third Avenue, was, in the words of one observer, "an untidy little person with rather ill-tended teeth." But, from behind his horn-rimmed spectacles, he looked out at the world with alert, questioning eyes and the ACLU's challenge was more than he could resist. On May 5, with Baldwin's offer of financial support in his pocket, he headed downtown to F. E. Robinson's drugstore where he promptly became involved with three members of the Dayton bar in an argument over the constitutionality of the Butler Act.

At this fortuitous moment, John Thomas Scopes, a 24-year-old graduate of the University of Kentucky, who had been doubling as science teacher and football coach at Dayton's Central High School, came into Robinson's for his usual afternoon soda. Here, in this bespectacled, towheaded biologist, whose father was, according to Clarence Darrow, a man who "brought up his family to have their own opinions and to stand by them," Rappelyea saw his chance to make good on his rash promise to the ACLU. It took the rest of the afternoon to persuade Scopes to go along with the idea but, before the drugstore conclave broke up that evening, Rappelyea was able to telegraph the ACLU that he had found his prospective defendant. The next morning, he received a wire from New York: "We will cooperate Scopes case with financial help, legal advice and publicity." The *State of Tennessee v. John Thomas Scopes* was under way.

Rappelyea didn't waste any time. As soon as Scopes had consented to be his guinea pig, he headed for the sheriff's office where he swore out a warrant for the young teacher's arrest. A deputy was sent to Robinson's drugstore where, after waiting patiently for Scopes to finish his third soda for the day, he arrested him. On May 10, three Dayton magistrates decided that there was enough evidence that Scopes had been teaching his students the theory of evolution to hold him for the action of the Rhea County Grand Jury which was scheduled to convene early in August. Bail was set at $1,000 and it was promptly posted by the ACLU.

To the merchants of Dayton, the impending trial was a bonanza of no mean proportions. It was sure to fill Main Street with thousands of curiosity seekers who could be counted on to leave many a sawbuck behind them. But more than that, if Dayton was ever to get on the map, this was its chance. For years it had been going downhill as Chattanooga, its neighbor to the southwest, had grown by leaps and bounds. With a monkey matched against the Bible in the newly painted brick courthouse that sat on a two-acre plot off Market Street, there was no telling what might be in store for the town.

But there was one disturbing cloud on the horizon. The possibilities of a wide-open antievolution trial had not been lost on Chattanoogans who began to press the city's official family to get the jump on Dayton. Judge John T. Raulston, of the 18th Circuit Court, who was slated to preside at the Scopes trial, spiked that one by calling a special session of the Grand Jury on May 25. After Rappelyea had been replaced by Walter White, the Rhea County superintendent of schools, as the complaining witness, the 13 jurors took less than an hour to indict Scopes whose trial was then set for Friday, July 10. Raulston had saved the day for the Main Street merchants who promptly organized eager committees to scrub and paint the town into a brightness it hadn't known since Peter Donaldson's blast furnace had failed in 1913. As one reporter put it, "Dayton was determined to be ready for its fame."

In Darrow's opinion, "the little town of Dayton, Tennessee, had never been heard of very far away from home." The seat of Rhea County, it was a prosperous village of some 2,000 residents, most of whom were gainfully employed by the four or five factories and mills that punctuated its outskirts. Every Saturday afternoon, the Cumberland Mountain farmers flocked into town to spend the money their wheat, tobacco and strawberry crops had earned for them. They would park their open Model-T Fords on the unpaved side streets and, after a snack at the Hotel Aqua, wander in and out of the shops that filled the brick and wooden buildings on Main and Market streets. On Sunday morning, almost the entire community could be found in the nine churches whose spires gave Dayton the nearest thing to a skyline it would ever have.

However, the town was far from a hotbed of religious fanatics. Although theology was always a lively subject on its shady street corners, the average Daytonian was not one to lose his head over sacerdotal differences of opinion. But its ministers didn't share their parishioners' equanimity on matters spiritual. Convinced, publicly at least, that "the Holy Bible contains and is itself the fountain of true wisdom," they set about raising the funds they hoped to donate to the prosecution staff to offset the $1,000 fees which, rumor had it, the ACLU was dangling before the eager noses of local lawyers. Scopes and any other evolutionist had to be shown that anyone who taught "our children any theory which has as its purpose or tendency the discrediting of our religion" would be promptly punished. If the Rev. L. M. Cartwright and his cohorts couldn't disprove Darwin's hypothesis, they could certainly discourage its converts.

When Scopes was first arrested, he had retained John Randolph Neal, a former law professor at the University of Tennessee, who had just opened a law school in Knoxville. Neal, despite his reputation for eccentricity, was astute enough to recognize that he lacked the trial experience that Scopes's defense demanded. Originally, he was convinced that John W. Davis was the right man to represent the young teacher but, when Clarence Darrow volunteered his services, Neal realized that the man and the case had met. "For the first, the last, and the only time in my life," Darrow later told a friend, "I volunteered my services in a case. I did this because I really wanted to take part in it."

What undoubtedly motivated Darrow to take this unprecedented — and, as it turned out, extremely expensive step — was the fact that, on May 13, William Jennings Bryan, the thrice-defeated Democrat candidate for the presidency, had announced in Pittsburgh that he would, Tennessee officialdom willing, represent the World's Christian Fundamentals Association in the case. Bryan, who was at the time a vociferous hawker for Florida real estate, was, in Darrow's opinion, "the logical man to prosecute the case." He had sparked the passage of antievolution statutes in several Bible Belt states and was the leader of the U.S. fundamentalist movement. Two years earlier, he and Darrow had clashed in the pages of the *Chicago Tribune* over what the Chicagoan considered the former's attempts "to shut out the teaching of science from the public schools." A Dayton booster could hardly have asked for a better cast.

On the evening of July 9, Darrow arrived in a Dayton that looked as if it were expecting a revival meeting rather than a criminal prosecution. As he drove from the railroad station, he passed under signs that admonished him to "Come to Jesus" and "Prepare to Meet Thy Maker." The town was bedecked with flags and bunting while sidewalk refreshment stands, with monkey posters pasted on their sides, lined both sides of Main Street. Two tame chimpanzees in a store window were entertaining the curious crowds that had been flocking into town for more than a week. Newspapermen, radio operators, photographers, farmers, telegraphers, preachers, beggars, tourists and unemployed coal miners — they all thronged into Dayton in such hordes that every available bed had been spoken for weeks before the trial was scheduled to get underway. If nothing else, the big show, which H. L. Mencken had already dubbed the "Monkey Trial," was sure to have an audience which would be as huge as it was diverse.

Darrow's first night in Dayton was spent in The Mansion, an abandoned plantation on the outskirts of town that Rappelyea, in a burst of sudden inspiration, had reopened for the occasion. But a man used to the conveniences of Chicago was not one to camp more than 12 hours in a house that lacked running water and the lawyer spent the rest of the trial in the home of one of the local bankers. Bryan, who had arrived two days before, was quartered at a private home from which he sallied forth to address, in quick succession, the Dayton Progressive Club, the Rhea County board of education, and the Methodist Episcopal Church South. In between, when he could tear himself away from the prodigious meals his hosts insisted on serving him, he posed for pictures with John Washington Butler, Judge Raulston, and every minister in town.

Friday, the 10th, dawned hot and humid. When Darrow arrived at the courthouse, he passed under a sign that proclaimed in large letters, "Read Your Bible." He walked up the rather steep stairs that led to the second-floor courtroom where Raulston, who liked to refer to himself as "jist a reg'lar mountin'eer jedge," was already esconced behind his newly painted bench. Darrow pushed his way slowly through the perspiring crowd that blocked every aisle in the courtroom. As he sank into the one vacant chair at the defense table, he nodded to Arthur Garfield Hays, Dudley Field Malone and John Randolph Neal, who were there to assist him. Across the way, at the prosecution table sat Bryan, his son, William, Jr., and five Tennessee lawyers of varying shapes and sizes. After the Rev. Mr. Cartwright had reminded everyone to look to God for "that wisdom to so transact the business of this court in such a way and manner as that Thy name may be honored and glorified among men," things were off and running.

But first a little repair work was necessary. The special Grand Jury that had originally indicted Scopes had been assembled so hurriedly that there was some doubt as to its legality. Raulston promptly swore in a new panel and began to read the Butler Act to it. Then he picked up his well-thumbed copy of the Bible and, in a voice that would have delighted Billy Graham, intoned the first 27 sections of Genesis, pausing significantly at those portions that insisted, "God created man in His own image." Three of Scopes's students then told the 13 bumpkins in the jury box that he had taught his classes all about evolution from George William Hunter's *Civic Biology*. In less than an hour, the defendant was properly charged and the prosecution was back on the rails.

The first order of business was the selection of the jury. There wasn't much to choose from since only 19 talesmen had shown up that morning. Darrow, who prided himself on his painstaking care in picking a panel, didn't waste much time with the bemused farmers who shuffled into the jury box and waited patiently for the agnostic from Chicago, to question them as to their qualifications. By 1:30 p.m. the jury was complete. Of its 11 members who attended church regularly, six were Baptists, four Methodists and one an adherent of the Disciples of Christ. The single backslider said that he perused the Bible from time to time, but not "like I ought to." At least one — a

former miner named Jim Riley — admitted he could not read but,
since both sides apparently considered illiteracy an asset, he was
promptly waved into the jury box. As the 12th man — S. S. Wright —
took his seat, Raulston, who was obviously in no hurry to rush the
trial along, announced that court would adjourn for the weekend.

On Monday, things began in earnest. After A. T. Stewart, the
attorney general for the 18th Judicial Circuit, had read the indictment to the jury, Neal immediately moved to dismiss it on the
ground that it violated both the state and federal constitutions.
Raulston thought that the legal arguments on these points might be
too heady for his back country jury — which had not yet been sworn
in — and he excused its members who promptly repaired to the
courthouse lawn where they eagerly listened to the proceedings over
the loudspeakers. After the lesser lights on both sides of the fence
had used up the morning in forensic fireworks, a now coatless
Darrow, who had just been dubbed a "Tennessee Colonel" by
Raulston, began his attack on the constitutionality of the Butler Act.

After assuring the judge that he would "always remember that
this court is the first one that ever gave me the great title of
'Colonel,' " he got down to the business at hand. First of all, he
turned to face Bryan, who was busy cooling himself with a palm fan,
and declared that the Great Commoner was the one "who is responsible for this foolish, mischievous and wicked act." Then he spent the
rest of the afternoon ripping into the antievolution law, which he
classified, "as bold an attempt to destroy learning as was ever made
in the Middle Ages." He had just gotten up a full head of steam when
Raulston interrupted him to announce that it was "adjourning time."
This pronouncement didn't seem to carry much weight with Darrow
who swept on to his climax:

> Today it is the public-school teachers, tomorrow the private. The
> next day the preachers and the lecturers, the magazines, the
> books, the newspapers. After a while, your Honor it is the setting
> of man against man and creed against creed until, with flying ban-
> ners, and beating drums, we are marching backward to the glori-
> ous ages of the 16th century when bigots lighted fagots to burn
> the men who dared to bring any intelligence, enlightenment and
> culture to the human mind.

As he sat down, he noticed for the first time that, in his excitement,
he had ripped one of his shirt sleeves.

The next morning — Tuesday, July 14 — he stormed back into the courtroom and shook Raulston to his back teeth by demanding that the practice of opening court with a prayer be abandoned: "I don't object to the jury or anyone else praying in secret or in private," he argued, "but I do object to the turning of this courtroom into a meetinghouse in the trial of this case. This case is a conflict between science and religion and no attempt should be made by means of prayer to influence the deliberation and consideration by the jury of the facts in this case." After Raulston had recovered his equilibrium, he informed Darrow that it had "been my custom since I have been a judge to have prayers in the courtroom when it was convenient, and I know of no reason why I should not follow up this custom, so I will overrule the objection." As a compromise, he asked New York's Rev. Charles Francis Potter, who had come to Dayton as a witness for the defense, to lead the next day's prayer.

Raulston spent the rest of the day working on his opinion which would accompany his decision on the defense motion to dismiss the indictment. However, at the very moment he was dictating it to his stenographer, the International News Service had [already] informed its subscribers that the defense motion would be denied. The judge, furious at being upstaged, appointed a committee of newspapermen, headed by Richard Beamish of the *Philadelphia Inquirer*, to investigate the leak. The committee's report was as simple as it was conclusive. It seemed that William K. Hutchison, an INS reporter, had asked Raulston whether the court would be adjourned to the next day after the opinion was read. When the judge replied that it would, Hutchison guessed that the motion had been denied and released a story to that effect. Raulston decided to let the matter drop with a warning to the newsmen not to "ask me any questions without giving me on notice as to what it is about."

On Wednesday morning, he confirmed Hutchison's accurate guesswork and announced that he would not quash the indictment. His reasons were simple — no one was forced to teach in the public schools and, if any teacher's conscience was troubled by having to hew to the letter of the Butler Act, he could resign and teach in a private institution. Why, if this law wasn't constitutional, the Holy Writ itself was suspect! He raced through his 6,000-word opinion in a little more than an hour, pausing only to wipe the perspiration from his face with a large scarlet handkerchief. When he had finished, the courthouse clock read 11:13 a.m. and he promptly adjourned for lunch.

That afternoon, Foreman Jack R. Thompson, a former U.S. Marshal, led his fellow jurors back into the box and, at long last, they were sworn in. Their first official act was to request, through their foreman, that the judge "take up the matter of some electric fans here." Unfortunately, the depleted state of the county treasury would not permit such an extravagance, but Raulston graciously consented to "divide my fan," and it was placed on an oblique angle with the jury box. He also suggested that a foraging squad be sent out to see what could be done about "borrowing" a fan or two in town.

The first witness for Bryan and company was Walter White, the county superintendent of schools, who had signed the second complaint against Scopes. He said that the defendant had admitted to him back in May that he had used Hunter's *Civic Biology* in class and that it was absolutely impossible to teach from it without presenting Darwin's theory. As for the Butler Act, Scopes had told White that "the law was unconstitutional anyway." Yet, despite the threat the text posed to the impressionable minds of Tennessee's small fry, it had been used in the state's school system since 1909 and had been officially adopted by the School Book Commission in 1924. In fact, it could be purchased in Dayton from the now celebrated drugstore of F. E. Robinson who, in addition to his pharmaceutical pursuits, was the president of the county board of education. When Darrow asked the witness if he had ever warned any teacher about the book's evil contents, or if anyone had ever complained to him about them, White's answer to the question was a drawled, "No, Sir."

When White stepped down from glory, he was followed by 14-year-old Howard Morgan, the son of Luke Morgan, of the Dayton Bank & Trust Company, to whose house Darrow and his wife, Ruby, had fled after one night's experience with The Mansion's inactive plumbing. Young Howard was one of Scopes's students. According to him, the defendant had insisted that "the earth was once a hot molten mass, too hot for plant or animal life to exist upon it; in the sea the earth cooled off; there was a little germ of a one-cell organism that formed and this organism kept on evolving until it got to be a pretty good-sized animal and then came on to be a land animal, and it kept on evolving, and from this was man, and that man was just another mammal."

Howard looked disappointed when Stewart looked over at Darrow and purred, "Your witness, Colonel," Under the Chicagoan's gentle questioning, the boy admitted that Scopes had never said, "a cat was the same as a man." On the contrary, "he said that man had reasoning power; these animals did not." After observing that he wasn't as sure as Scopes about that, Darrow asked the witness whether he could remember anything else of a salacious nature that the defendant had taught him. Howard could not.

Seventeen-year-old Harry Shelton backed up his classmate's story. Yes, Scopes had indeed said that man was descended from a lower order of animals, but what he had learned hadn't had any adverse effect on him. He still went to church regularly, just as he had before he was told that "all life comes from a single cell." Darrow, who looked quite satisfied with the way things were going, asked Harry, "Did Mr. Scopes teach you that man came from the monkey?" As the boy opened his mouth to answer the question, there was a horrendous shriek from the direction of the courthouse lawn. A chimpanzee, brought from New York as a publicity stunt, had just been struck by a rock propelled by the slingshot of a small boy who quite obviously had little respect for his ancestors. Harry Shelton's answer to Darrow's question was never to be recorded by the thoroughly distracted court stenographer. It had been in F. E. Robinson's emporium that what Scopes called "just a drugstore discussion that got past control" started all the hullabaloo. Robinson, who presided over the county school board, had been present while Rappelyea was trying to convince Scopes to throw himself in the path of the antievolution law. Yes, he had heard the defendant state that he had been teaching Darwin's theory to his biology class. In fact, John Scopes had gone even further and said that it was impossible to

A chimpanzee, brought from New York as a publicity stunt, had just been struck by a rock propelled by the slingshot of a small boy...

teach the subject from any of the available books without violating the Butler Act.

But Robinson, whose drugstore sold everything from sassafras to hickory chips, also purveyed Hunter's *Civic Biology*. Darrow reminded him that he might be talking himself into a criminal prosecution but, as Stewart informed Raulston, "the law says 'teach,' not sell."

They were still laughing at that one in the back rows when Robinson proudly admitted that he had a monopoly on the book in Dayton and that copies were supplied to him by the county library in Chattanooga. No, he hadn't noticed "any signs of moral deterioration in the community" since he'd been selling them.

This was Tennessee's case against John Thomas Scopes. After those *pro forma* [defense] motions to dismiss the indictment had been denied, Darrow called his first witness, a bespectacled gentleman who turned out to be Dr. Maynard M. Metcalf, a zoologist from John Hopkins University, who described himself as an "evolutionist." He was the first of a band of scientific witnesses whom Darrow had brought to Dayton with him to show "what evolution is... and the interpretation of the Bible that prevails with men of intelligence who have studied it." But none of them were ever able to say their pieces. Bryan, in his one speech of the trial, convinced Raulston, who was ready to meet him more than halfway, that "the Bible, the record of the Son of God, the Savior of the World, born of the Virgin Mary, crucified and risen again — the Bible is not going to be driven out of this court by experts who come hundreds of miles to testify that they can reconcile evolution and its ancestors in the jungle, with man made by God in His image and put here for His purpose as part of a divine plan." Not very legal, perhaps, but quite persuasive.

Raulston, however, did consent to the submission of affidavits by Darrow's experts for the "information of the judge." When Darrow asked for the rest of the day to prepare these statements, Raulston indicated that he wasn't inclined to grant the request. "I do not understand," Darrow barked at him, "why every request of the State and every suggestion of the prosecution should meet with an endless loss of time; yet a bare suggestion of anything that is perfectly competent on our part should be immediately overruled." Raulston, with a bland smile, expressed the hope that "you do not mean to reflect upon the court?"

> Darrow: Well, your Honor, one has the right to hope.
> Raulston: I have the right to do something else perhaps.
> Darrow: All right, all right.

The next morning, Saturday the 18th, the *Chattanooga News* prophesized that Raulston would probably cite Darrow for contempt, when court reconvened after the weekend.

But on Monday the weather was much too hot for fireworks and

Darrow, after being cited, mollified the ruffled feelings of his Honor by admitting that "I went further than I should have gone and I want to apologize to the court for it." Raulston was more than magnanimous. "I accept Colonel Darrow's apology," he murmured. "I am sure his remarks were not premeditated. I am sure that if he had time to have thought and deliberated, he would not have spoken those words... We forgive him and we forget it and we command him to go back home and learn in his heart the words of the man who said: 'If you thirst, come unto Me and I will give thee life.' " Pyrrhus would have understood.

That afternoon, as the usual crowd of slightly more than 1,000 people pushed into the courtroom after the noon recess, a worried bailiff informed Raulston that there was some danger that the building would collapse. The latter decided to transfer the trial to the courthouse lawn, where an impromptu platform had been built to accommodate Bryan and the ministers, who had been using their free time to put in a word for the Bible and its copyright owner. But, from the defense's point of view, the courtroom *en plein air* had one drawback — there was a large sign on the courthouse wall facing the jurors, which importuned them to "Read Your Bible Daily." When Darrow suggested that a companion placard stating "Read Your Evolution" be erected alongside the offending sign, Raulston promptly decided to remove all signs. *Sic transit gloria mundi.*

After the furor had died down, Arthur Garfield Hays finished reading the statements that had been prepared by the scientists and clergymen Darrow had brought to Dayton, whose testimonies had been excluded by Raulston's ruling. Seven geologists, anthropologists and zoologists, as well as three Protestant ministers and a Jewish rabbi were represented as Hays, in a tired voice, tried his best to educate an increasingly exasperated Raulston. When the defense attorney had finished his readings, he offered into evidence two Bibles and sat down. Darrow whispered something in his ear, and Hays was back on his feet again. "The defense desires to call Mr. Bryan as a witness," he announced. "We should want to take Mr. Bryan's testimony for the purposes of our record, even if your Honor thinks it is not admissible in general, so we wish to call him now."

Despite Bryan's obvious discomfiture at having to take the stand, there was no escape. He was being called as an expert on the Bible, a status he had assumed before Chautauquas up and down the land, and he simply could not refuse to accept Darrow's challenge. After gaining a few minutes to collect his thoughts, by insisting that the lawyers for the defense be ordered to take the stand when he was finished, Bryan perched himself in the spindle-legged chair that passed for a witness chair. What the *New York Times* later described as the most amazing court scene in Anglo-Saxon history was about to be launched.

With the observation that he was sure the witness would tell the truth, Darrow waived having Bryan sworn. Then he got down to cases. He asked Bryan whether he had given considerable study to the Bible, and the old Democrat assured him that he had, "for about 50 years." With slight exceptions, Bryan was convinced that everything in the Scriptures should be taken literally. "When I read that a big fish swallowed Jonah," he bellowed, "I believe it, and I believe in a God who can make a whale and can make a man and make them both do what he pleases. One miracle is just as easy to believe as another."

As Darrow led his perspiring adversary through the Bible, from Creation to the Battle of Jericho, many of the reporters, sprawled on the benches that had been placed under the square's maple trees, remembered that he had asked many of the same questions in the pages of the *Chicago Tribune* two years earlier. Bryan had refused to answer them then, but he was forced to do so now. When the long day drew to a close, Bryan was a defeated and humiliated man, who had left whatever reputation he had brought into Dayton among the empty pop bottles and cracker jack boxes that littered the courthouse lawn. As Will Rogers put it, "he might make Tennessee the side show of America, but he can't make a street carnival of the whole United States."

With Bryan committed to defending the literalness of every incredible occurrence in the Bible, Darrow's task was a comparatively simple one. A man who believed that Joshua made the sun stand still, or that Eve was created out of Adam's rib, or that a giant flood destroyed all life on earth, was a sitting duck for an experienced and shrewd cross-examiner. As the day wore on, it was quite apparent that Bryan's answers were destroying him, even in the eyes of his friends, and that Darrow had succeeded in turning a rout into what had all the earmarks of a shattering victory.

Bryan's observation that he was "more interested in the Rock of Ages than the age of rocks" set the tone of the entire interrogation. For example, when Darrow took up the subject of Eve's temptation, the witness was certain that labor pains had originated with God's wrath at apple larceny.

Q. And for that reason, every woman born of woman who has to carry on the race, has childbirth pains because Eve tempted Adam in the Garden of Eden?

A. I will believe just what the Bible says. I ask you to put that in the language of the Bible, for I prefer that to your language. Read the Bible and I will answer.

Q. All right, I will do that: "And I will put enmity between thee and the woman" — that is referring to the serpent?

A. The serpent.

Q. " '…and between thy seed and her seed; it shall bruise thy head, and thou shalt bruise his heel.' Unto the woman he said, 'I will greatly multiply thy sorrow and thy conception; in sorrow thou shalt bring forth children; and thy desire shall be to thy husband and he shall rule over thee.' " That is right, is it?

A. I accept it as it is.

Q. And you believe that came about because Eve tempted Adam to eat the fruit?

A. Just as it says.

Q. As for the serpent, he had to "crawl upon his belly" for his nefarious part in the episode. Do you think that is why the serpent is compelled to crawl on his belly?

A. I believe that.

Q. Have you any idea how the snake went before that time?

A. No, sir.

Q. Do you know whether he walked on his tail or not?

A. No, sir. I have no way to know.

The laughter that accompanied Darrow's last question about the earthbound snake marked the beginning of the end. A few minutes earlier Bryan had admitted that the six days of Creation did not amount to "six days of 24 hours." His impression was that "they were periods" but he had no idea as to their length. The defender of the Word, who had refused to question Joshua's sun-stopping maneuver or Jonah's sojourn in the alimentary canal of a whale, knew that it took more than a week to build a makeshift barn, and somehow couldn't swallow a six-day Creation. But as far as the fundamentalists on the courthouse lawn were concerned, he had betrayed them all. When he walked home later that afternoon, only one man accompanied him. The rest of the crowd followed Darrow all the way to the Morgan house.

The next morning dawned cool and rainy, and Raulston ordered the circus back into the courthouse, cracks or not. After expunging

Bryan's testimony, because he felt it could "shed no light upon any issues that will be pending before the higher courts," he ordered the jury, which had been cooling its collective heels for more than a week just inside loudspeaker range, to get back to work. Darrow said that he thought it would save a great deal of time if the judge would instruct [the jury] to bring back a verdict of guilty so that the case could "get to a higher court." At 11:14 a.m. Wednesday, July 22, Captain Thompson led his colleagues down the stairs to the court-house lawn where, after some eight minutes of palaver and one ballot, they found Scopes guilty of violating the Butler Act. As to the fine, they were willing to leave that to Raulston, who had told them in advance that he intended to fix it at $100, the minimum under the statute.

The judge was as good as his word. He asked Scopes to stand up and informed him that he was indebted to the state of Tennessee in the sum of 100 singles. When Neal reminded Raulston that he had forgotten to ask the defendant whether he had anything to say before being sentenced, the judge was all apologies. The thin, bald-ing teacher, who had been silent for 12 sweltering days, didn't take very long to say what he had to say. "Your Honor, I feel that I have been convicted of violating an unjust statute. I will continue in the future, as I have in the past, to oppose the law in any way I can. Any other action would be in violation of my ideal of academic freedom — that is, to teach the truth — as guaranteed in our constitution, of personal and religious freedom. I think the fine is unjust."

Not to be outdone, his Honor, after imposing the fine again, told Scopes that "it sometimes takes courage to search diligently for a truth that may destroy our preconceived notions and ideas. It sometimes takes courage to declare a truth or stand for an act that is in contra-vention to the public sentiment. A man who is big enough to search for the truth and find it and declare it in the face of all opposition is a big man." While Darrow, Hays and Malone were digesting that one, the *Baltimore Sun* posted the $500 bond required as a condition of appeal and everyone began to congratulate everyone else. After Hays had promised to send the judge a copy of *Origin of Species*, Raulston said, "We will adjourn and Brother Jones will pronounce the benedic-tion." The first stage of *Tennessee v. John Thomas Scopes* was over.

For weeks before the trial, Bryan had been busy writing an antievolution speech which he looked forward to delivering in the courtroom. But Darrow's carefully planned capitulation on the trial's last day had deprived him of his national forum. Such a speech, however, could not remain locked up in the frustrated soul of a veteran Chautauquian who was not in the habit of keeping his thoughts to himself. After trying excerpts out on roadside audiences in Jasper and Winchester, Tennessee, he persuaded the *Chattanooga News* to publish it. But he was never to see it in print. On Sunday, July 26, he died of what Darrow, with more candor than good taste, termed "indigestion caused by over-eating." As for the great oration, Mrs. Bryan released it for general publication two days after her husband's death. It went largely unnoticed.

Everything else was anticlimatic. A year and a half later, the Tennessee Supreme Court sustained the constitutionality of the Butler Act. But its four members reversed Scopes's conviction because Raulston had violated the state constitution when he, and not the jury, had fixed the fine. Unless the prosecution insisted on bringing Scopes to trial again, the case was cold turkey, and Chief Justice Green did his best to keep it that way. "We see nothing to be gained," he urged, "by prolonging the life of this bizarre case." The attorney general took the rather broad hint Green had dropped, and immediately nolle prossed the indictment.

Although the school board offered to reinstate Scopes, he decided to take advantage of his notoriety and accepted a graduate scholarship. As for the Butler Act, it was never to be enforced again — in Tennessee or anywhere else for that matter. In 1951, a bill proposing its repeal was introduced by, of all people, Rhea County's representative in the Tennessee Legislature, but it was soundly defeated. Another attempt, 10 years later, was voted down, 69 to 17, in the House of Representatives. Today, it still lurks in the statute books, a remembrance of things past. But as far as the "victorious defeat" that clipped its wings was concerned, Darrow never grew tired of saying, "I believed that the cause was worthwhile, and was always glad that I helped."

The Scottsboro Nine
Alabama v. Haywood Patterson

On March 25, 1931, Victoria Price and Ruby Bates claimed they were gang-raped by 12 African American men on a Memphis-bound train. Nine young black men on the train were arrested and charged with the crime. Twelve days later, their trial took place at Scottsboro, Alabama. Their defense attorney was an alcoholic, who was drunk throughout the trial. The prosecutor on the other hand, told the jury, "Guilty or not, let's get rid of these niggers." After three days, all nine men were found guilty: eight, including two aged 14, were sentenced to death. The youngest, who was only thirteen, was given life imprisonment.

Although Ruby Bates testified at the second trial that the rape story had been invented by Victoria Price and that the crime had never taken place, the men were again found guilty. A third trial ended in the same result but a fourth in 1936 resulted in four of the men being acquitted. Four more were released in the 1940s, but the last prisoner, Andy Wright, had to wait until 1950 — 19 years after his arrest in Alabama — before achieving his freedom. The nine men were finally pardoned in 1976, yet only Clarence Norris (who spent 15 years in prison for the crime) was still alive. In 1977, the Alabama House Judiciary Committee rejected a proposal to pay Norris $10,000 in compensation for his time spent in prison.

The way the Scottsboro boys, as they became known, were defended is significant. The International Labor Defense (ILD) secured massive national and international publicity and built a mass defense campaign in the United States. Poems, short stories and plays were composed in support of the men and gained worldwide circulation.

This mass campaign eventually saved their lives. When the courtroom is far from neutral, the battle for justice must be fought in the streets as well. African Americans and whites together, mostly members of the Communist Party, gained access to churches and clubs in the community and spread the word about the case. They said a fair trial was impossible and mobilized mass pressure from Paris to South Africa, where demonstrations against U.S. racial injustice were held.

The Scottsboro case, a horrific "legal" example of the "southern justice" and klan-type terror of the time, is not just of "historical interest." As a group African Americans have been accused and imprisoned at far greater rates than the general populace, a situation that continues today.

Michael Smith

In 1931, Huntsville was a rickety industrial town in the northern reaches of Alabama. Most of its 30,000 inhabitants depended on one or another of the seven mills that were just beginning to be hit by the depression that had already paralyzed other parts of the country. By March, Margaret Mill, for example, had cut its working week to two days and its average daily wage to $1.20.

One of Margaret Mill's employees was a 17-year-old girl named Ruby Bates whose nomadic family lived in a shack on Depot Street, Huntsville's Negro section. The only whites on the block, the Bateses had migrated to Huntsville from the cotton fields of central Alabama. Sharecropping had not brought in enough to feed five mouths and, after Mr. Bates had deserted his brood and left for parts unknown, Ruby and her mother decided to move into a town where both women could work at one of the mills. First it was Athens and then Huntsville.

Monday, March 23, 1931, was a sunny day on the cool side. Ruby, who hadn't worked for more than a week, was standing near her front window, watching her brother and sister playing with the Negro children on Depot Street, when Victoria Price, a Margaret coworker, strolled up the front walk. Twenty-five-year-old Victoria, who lived with her mother on Arms Street, supplemented her meager mill earnings with some slack-time prostitution. By 1931, she had a sizable arrest record even though Walter Sanders, Huntsville's deputy sheriff, described her as "a quiet prostitute [who] don't go rarin' around cuttin' up in public."

Victoria had an idea. Jack Tiller, her current boyfriend, had run into Lester Carter who had just been released from a Huntsville chain gang. The two men had suggested that Victoria find a girl for

Lester and then they would shake the Alabama dust from their feet. Ruby was more than willing [to be that girl] and, after packing her few belongings, hurried over to the Price's two-room shack where Tiller and Carter were waiting. Both girls had on overalls, under which they were wearing their entire wardrobes. The two couples spent the night in a nearby hobo jungle where, between some semi-public lovemaking, they made plans to go west and "hustle the towns."

But, in the cold light of dawn, Tiller suddenly realized that he had a wife who might not take too kindly to his proposed cross-country tour with Victoria, and decided to give up the venture and go home. Carter and the girls jumped a freight for Chattanooga, almost 100 miles away, where they bedded down in some woods just outside of the city. There they were joined by a street poet named Orville Gilley, otherwise known as "Carolina Slim," who was swiftly enlisted as a replacement for Tiller. At 11:00 the next morning, the quartet boarded a 40-car freight, which was bound for Memphis. They settled down in an open gondola car that was almost filled to the gunwales with crushed rock. Five other white boys were sitting at the opposite end of the car.

The freight, which was following the tracks of the Southern Railroad, crossed into Alabama at Bridgeport, and passed through Stevenson, Fackler, Hollywood, Scottsboro, Lim Rock and Woodville before it came to a stop at Paint Rock, less than 30 miles east of Huntsville. Shortly after Gilley, Carter and the two girls had boarded the gondola, the train stopped for water at a siding in Stevenson. Seconds later, a dozen or so colored boys climbed into the gondola from an adjoining box car. A fight immediately ensued between the invaders and the seven white boys in the gondola, the net result of which was the forcible eviction of all the whites with the exception of Gilley.

The boys who had been thrown off the slowly moving train limped back into Stevenson where they reported the incident to the stationmaster. He telephoned ahead to Paint Rock, some 38 miles west of Stevenson, and, when the train pulled into that northern Alabama hamlet at 2:30 p.m., a posse of 75 armed white men was waiting for it. Nine Negro boys between 13 and 20 years of age, as well as Ruby Bates, Victoria Price and Orville Gilley, were removed from the gondola. The girls were taken to a doctor's office for a physical examination while the Negroes were locked up in Scottsboro's tiny jailhouse. When an ugly crowd began to gather, Sheriff M. L. Wann asked

Governor B. M. Miller to send in the National Guard. The troops arrived at 4:00 the next morning and escorted the nine suspects to Gadsden, Alabama. Four days later, they were returned to Scottsboro where they were all indicted on the charge that they "forcibly ravished... a woman against the peace and dignity of the state of Alabama."

Their trials started on Monday, April 6, 1931, in the Jackson County Circuit Court. H. G. Bailey, the state solicitor, asked Judge Alf E. Hawkins to sever [separate] the trials, a request that was promptly granted. Charlie Weems and Clarence Norris, who were 20 and 19 respectively, were tried first; their trial was followed by that of 18-year-old Haywood Patterson. The third involved five boys — Andy Wright (19), Willie Roberson (17), Olen Montgomery (17), Ozie Powell (16) and Eugene Williams (15). The youngest defendant, 13-year-old Roy Wright, was to stand trial by himself.

The boys' pedigrees were much the same. They were all destitute, illiterate and unskilled southern Negroes who came from Tennessee and Georgia. Roberson was suffering from both gonorrhea and syphilis while Montgomery was practically blind. According to Patterson, "All nine of us were riding the freight for the same reason, to go somewhere and find work." These were the "nine black fiends" who, according to the *Jackson County Sentinel* of March 26, 1931, had "committed [the] revolting crime."

When the trials started, none of the defendants was in any position to retain an attorney. Judge Hawkins had appointed "all members of the bar for the purpose of arraigning the defendants, and then, of course, I anticipated them to continue to help if no counsel appears." A Stephen W. Roddy, a Chattanooga lawyer, who had been approached by members of the National Association for the Advancement of Colored People, told Hawkins that, although he had not been paid and would not "appear as counsel," he was willing to do what he could on the defendants' behalf. He was joined by Milo Moody, a member of the Scottsboro bar, who expressed his willingness "to help Mr. Roddy in anything I can do about it under the circumstances." The judge was quite obviously relieved that the niceties of justice would be scrupulously observed.

Roddy's first step was to present a petition signed with nine X's asking for a change of venue. In view of the hostile crowd that filled the courthouse lawn, he insisted that a fair trial was impossible in Scottsboro. Bailey made it quite clear that he considered Roddy's suggestion impertinent and called Major Joe Starnes, the command-ing officer of the National Guard, to rebut it. Starnes assured the court that "the crowd was here out of curiosity and not as a hostile demonstration toward these defendants." The major's opinion was enough for Hawkins and he overruled Roddy's motion.

The four trials were over by Thursday morning. On Friday, eight of the Negroes were sentenced to die in the Kilby Prison electric chair early the following July. Because one juror refused to vote for Roy Wright's execution, his trial resulted in a hung jury. But eight out of nine was a good batting average in anybody's league and the crowd outside the courthouse, which sang "There'll be a Hot Time in the Old Town Tonight" as each guilty verdict was announced, was more than satisfied with the week's work.

In all four trials, Victoria Price and Ruby Bates were the witness-es-in-chief for the prosecution. Their stories left little to be desired as far as the state solicitor was concerned. After the Negroes had invaded the gondola car, they had cowed the white boys by "telling them that they would kill them, that it was their car and we were their women from now on." Victoria accused Norris of having "sexu-al intercourse with me" while Weems threatened her with a .45 pis-tol and a knife. Norris had "pulled my overalls over me" and "the lit-tle one, the smallest one, was holding my legs." She claimed Norris had not only raped her, but stolen her knife, $1.50 of her money, and a pocket handkerchief. Twelve Negroes had entered the gon-dola car but "three got off." She denied that she was travelling with any of the seven white boys who had been involved in the fight at Stevenson. In all, she and Ruby had each been raped by six boys but "three of hers got away."

Ruby said that the Negroes had ordered the white boys in the gondola car "to unload" before the rapes took place. Then, while some of the defendants threatened her with knives and pistols, she had been thrown to the gravel-covered floor of the car and attacked. "There were three Negroes to each girl," she told the spellbound jury, "one for intercourse, one for holding the knife and one for holding the pistol. They never did remove the knife or pistol."

Two physicians — Drs. R. R. Bridges and M. H. Lynch — had examined both girls a little more than an hour after they had been removed from the train. Although he had found no "recent lacera-tions" on either woman, Bridges said that he had "found semen in the vagina of each one." Two years later, he was to state that "the semen did not move and we don't swear as to whether it is dead or alive unless we see it move." No lacerations, tears or bruises were found in the genital region of either girl. Both Victoria and Ruby had seemed quite calm during Bridge's first examination but when he visited them in jail the next day they were somewhat hysterical. Lynch, who was the head of the Jackson County Health Department, confirmed his colleague's observations.

Hawkins, who was determined to get the trials over with as soon as possible, refused to let Roddy and Moody do more than present a token defense. Nowhere was this more apparent than in their cross-examination of the two physicians. When they tried to show that Victoria and Ruby were far from virgins, the judge said such evidence was irrelevant. While Dr. Bridges was on the stand, Roddy asked him whether either girl showed any indications of gonorrhea or syphilis. Hawkins refused to let the physician answer the question despite the fact that Willie Roberson was suffering from both diseases. Although Bridges confirmed that Roberson had "a bad case of it," he was sure that "it is possible for him to have intercourse."

Lynch and Bridges were followed by a number of Stevenson residents who had seen the fight on the gondola car. Luther Morris had been in a barn loft, some 30 yards away from the Southern roadbed, when the train passed. He had seen a "bunch of Negroes put off five white men and take charge of two white girls. The two white girls were doing their best to jump and the Negroes got the two white girls and they were pulled back down in the car." Two of the boys who had been thrown off the train by the Negroes passed by Morris's barn on their way to Stevenson but were too stunned to talk to him. "They just said: 'I am dying…' they were badly hurt."

Orry Robbins had been standing near a woodpile, a hundred yards away from the tracks, when the train passed. He said that "I saw two girls and these colored people… one of the colored men grabbed a woman and threw her down." T. L. Dobbins, who was only a few feet away from the train, had observed the scuffling in the gondola car but, as far as the participants were concerned, he "could not tell whether they were white or black." Lee Adams, who was 200 yards away, had watched "a bunch of people in a car… striking and about that time I saw someone go over the top of the car." Later, he saw two of the boys who had been thrown off the train running toward Stevenson and "the blood was running down their faces." By the time the train passed Sam Mitchell, it was going between 30 and 40 miles per hour. As for the fight, "we see'd them wrestlin', 'peared like. That's all I seen; the train was going pretty fast."

When the train stopped at Paint Rock, the armed posse was waiting for it. Bailey used some of its members to add what little they could to the case against the defendants. Tom Taylor Rousseau was certain that Victoria "was unconscious" when "they toted her off the train. She had her eyes closed and was lying over this way… she was in no condition to walk." Victoria had previously testified that, "I was unconscious after I got off the train… I became unconscious when I fell off the stirrup on the side of the gondola." T. M. Latham, a deputy sheriff, testified that the girl "could not walk" when he first saw her. Jim Broadway said, "The Bates girl seemed to be in fairly good shape but the other could not hardly talk and couldn't walk."

Both women told Latham that "we have been mistreated" but Broadway, who was only a few feet away, said, "I did not hear Victoria Price make no complaint, either to me or to anyone else about the treatment they received at the hands of these defendants over there." Victoria herself had admitted that the defendants' arrest had not been "on account of any complaint of mine." Lastly, Jackson County Deputy Sheriff Arthur W. Woodall testified that he had found Victoria's penknife in Norris' pocket.

Orville Gilley, who was the only white boy who had not been thrown off the train as it pulled out of Stevenson, was used in the third trial. Outside of the girls, he was the sole white eyewitness to what had occurred in the gondola car. Yet Bailey used him only for the limited purpose of identifying five of the defendants as having been present in the car. "I saw those five in the car… every one of those five in the gondola."

> Q. Were the girls in there?
> A. Yes, sir.

Evidently, Sam Gilley's son had been singularly unconcerned with what was happening to his traveling companions for he made no attempt either to notify the engineer or the conductor or to leave the train.

When the state rested, all of the defendants took the stand. Weems accused Haywood Patterson of forcing him, at the point of a pistol, to fight the white boys on the train. But he insisted that he "didn't see the girls. I never did see the girls… If anybody had anything to do with the girls, I don't know nothing about it." Clarence Norris on the other hand, had "seen every one of them have something to do with those girls, all eight of them, but I didn't." According to him, Patterson had said, "he was going over there to run the white boys off and going to have something to do with them." Patterson swore that he had been sitting on the box car behind the gondola, from which vantage point he had seen Weems and several others rape Victoria. "But I had nothing to do with those girls," he insisted. Roy Wright also said that "there was nine Negroes down there with the girls and all had intercourse with them... I saw that with my own eyes."

The other defendants insisted that they were completely innocent. They denied that they had seen the girls until the freight stopped at Paint Rock. Ozie Powell "never did see the girls" from the time he boarded the freight at Chattanooga until it was stopped at Paint Rock. Olen Montgomery, who claimed that he had been "back in the seventh car from the end of the train... by my lonely... first saw them at Paint Rock," and Eugene Williams "did not see the girls at all until we got to Paint Rock." Andy Wright swore that "I did not have intercourse with a woman on that train" while Willie Roberson testified that, because of his venereal diseases, "I am not able to have sexual intercourse."

After the eight convicted defendants had been sent to the Kilby Prison death row, Roddy filed four motions for new trials. Among other grounds, he urged that the defendants were not given sufficient time in which to prepare their defense and that the atmosphere in Scottsboro was so hostile that a fair trial was impossible. On June 22, Hawkins denied all the motions and, in Kilby's Cell 222, Haywood Patterson "was busy living from minute to minute" while he and the Scottsboro boys, as they came to be called, were waiting for their July 10 date with current supplied free of charge by the Alabama Light and Power Company.

But July 10 came and went and the only man executed at Kilby that night was one Will Stokes, an ax-murderer, who went to his death a few minutes after midnight. An appeal to the Alabama Supreme Court from Judge Hawkin's refusal to grant new trials had resulted in a stay of execution for Patterson & Company. It wasn't until the following spring that the judgments were affirmed and seven of the defendants were resentenced to die on May 13, 1932. Because Eugene Williams was under 16, Alabama law required that he be tried as a juvenile delinquent and his conviction was reversed on that ground alone.

When the appeals were argued before the Alabama Supreme Court, neither Roddy's nor Moody's names appeared on the briefs for the defendants. George W. Chamlee, Sr., and his son, George, Jr., two Chattanooga lawyers, now represented the Scottsboro boys. They had been selected by the International Labor Defense (ILD), a communist affiliate devoted to defending any member of the "working class" who ran afoul of "capitalist justice." Through Joseph R. Brodsky, its general counsel, it had financed the appeals to Alabama's highest court.

On April 9, 1932, the judges refused to rehear the appeals and it looked very much as if the year-long fight to save eight nondescript lives was about over. But the ILD was not one to leave any stone unturned (or unhurled) and it asked the U.S. Supreme Court to intervene. Early in October, Walter H. Pollak, another ILD attorney, argued in Washington that the defendants had not received a fair and impartial trial; had been denied the right of counsel and sufficient time in which to prepare their defense, and had been tried before juries from which qualified Negroes were deliberately excluded.

On November 7, 1932, seven of the nine justices reversed the convictions and ordered new trials for all the defendants. In their opinion, the Scottsboro Boys had not been given an opportunity to secure counsel of their own choice. "Not only was that not done here, but such designation of counsel as was attempted was either so indefinite or too close upon the trial as to amount to a denial of effective and substantial aid... We hold that the defendants were not accorded the right of counsel in any substantial sense. To decide otherwise, would simply be to ignore actualities."

After the first trials, Ruby Bates had returned to Depot Street. On January 5, 1933, she sat down at the kitchen table and wrote a letter to a "Dearest Earl," evidently a successor in interest to Lester Carter. In it, she told him that "those Negroes did not touch me or those white boys... i know it was wrong too let those Negroes die on account of me i hope you will believe my statement because it is the gods truth... i wish those Negroes are not Burnt on account of me." The messenger to whom she gave the letter never delivered it. Ten minutes after he started out, he was in the Huntsville lockup, accused of starting a street fight. The police turned the letter over to the prosecution and it took the ILD until the end of January to get a court order permitting its attorneys to photostat it.

On March 6, a motion for a change of venue was granted by Judge Hawkins and Decatur was selected as the *mise en scène* in a case that was now as well known in Berlin and Paris as it was in Birmingham and Memphis. A week later, William Patterson, the ILD's executive secretary, persuaded Samuel S. Leibowitz, who, at 39, was New York's best known criminal lawyer, to come south and see what he could do to convince 12 Morgan County jurymen to give "this poor scrap of colored humanity a fair, square deal." Act II was about to begin.

In Kilby's death row, Guard L. J. Burrs told the defendants to get ready for a trip to town. On the first day of spring, they were taken to the Jefferson County Jail in Birmingham to await their second trials. Six days later, Patterson's began in Decatur's white-columned courthouse before Judge James E. Horton who, according to the defendant, "looked like pictures of Abe Lincoln." This was to be no one-day outing. To counteract Leibowitz, Thomas Knight, Jr., Alabama's attorney general, with State Solicitor Bailey and Morgan County Circuit Solicitor Wade Wright at his elbow, entered the lists for Alabama. On March 27, Horton granted the state's motion to sever Patterson's case from those of the other defendants and, on the following morning, his trial was off and running.

Leibowitz's opening gambit was to move to dismiss the indictment because Negroes had been systematically excluded from the Grand Jury rolls of Jackson County. According to Section 8603 of the Alabama Code, all male citizens between the ages of 21 and 65 who could read English and had not been convicted of any offense involving moral turpitude could serve on grand and petit juries if they were "generally reputed to be honest and intelligent men, and are esteemed in the community for their integrity, good character and sound judgment." Literacy could be waived if the prospective juror was a "freeholder or householder."

As far as grand juries were concerned, evidently not one of the more than 600 adult male Negroes in Jackson County had ever met the requirements of Section 8603. Jefferson E. Moody, a member of the Jury Commission from 1930 to 1931, couldn't remember seeing any Negroes on the list. C. A. Wann, who had been clerk of the Circuit Court for five years, said, "I do not know of one single instance where a Negro had served on a Grand Jury in Jackson County, in all my experience." Hamlin Caldwell, a court reporter for the Ninth Judicial Circuit, who hadn't missed a session in Jackson

County for 24 years, testified that he had "never seen a colored man on the Grand Jury…" J. S. Benson was the editor of *Progressive Age*, a Scottsboro newspaper. Convinced that no Negro could possibly qualify as a grand juror ("They all steal"), he had "never known of a single instance where any Negroes were put on the jury roll."

Then the defense called a number of Jackson County Negroes who seemed to meet the standards of 8603. John Sandford, a 50-year-old plasterer, who could read and write and had no criminal record, swore that he had "never been put on a jury roll and have never been examined by any Jury Commission as to my qualifications…" He said that he knew a great many eligible Negroes in the county who had also never been called for jury service. Mark Taylor, who was a member of the District No. 88 School Board, and Travis Mosely, who owned real property in Scottsboro, told similar stories. Finally, after Leibowitz had paraded five other seemingly qualified Negroes to the stand, Horton called it quits and denied the defense motion to dismiss the indictment.

Then Leibowitz turned to another track. Anticipating a second conviction, he decided to lay a more substantial foundation for an eventual return to Washington and attacked the Morgan County petit jury system as well. First, he called a great many Decatur Negroes who clearly met all the statutory requirements to sit on juries. Among others, there were Dr. Frank Sykes, a dentist; Dr. N. E. Cashin, a physician; Rev. L. B. Womack, the pastor of the First Missionary Baptist Church; and J. E. Pickett, a teacher in the Negro High School for more than 18 years. He followed them with Arthur J. Tidwell, a member of the Jury Board of the Morgan County, who stated, "I have never seen a Negro serve on a jury, never heard of one." Neither had his two fellow commissioners.

When Leibowitz threatened to call every person whose name appeared on the jury roll "even if it breaks the state" and requested subpoenas for almost 400 other Morgan County Negroes, Judge Horton gave up the ghost and conceded that it looked as if Alabama deliberately excluded Negroes from its juries. With these preliminaries out of the way, an all-white jury was impaneled and Victoria Price, "in dress-up clothes," sashayed up to the witness stand. In 12 minutes, she repeated much the same story she had told in Scottsboro, a year back.

Victoria proved to be more than a match for Leibowitz. When he pointed to a 32-ft. model of the freight train, which he had brought with him from New York and asked her to point out the gondola car, she spiked his guns by mumbling, "The gondola I was in was much bigger than that thing." Since she had sworn at Scottsboro that she was 21 when the defendants raped her, he asked her whether it wasn't true that she was actually four years older. "I ain't that educated that I can figure it out." When he accused her of being "a little bit of an actress," she snapped back, "You're a pretty good actor yourself."

As her cross-examination developed, it was apparent that the defense was staking everything on getting Victoria to admit that she had invented the rape story in order to keep from being arrested for traveling across the Alabama-Tennessee line with Carter and Gilley. This, the witness passed off as "some of that Ruby Bates dope." After Ruby's letter to "Dearest Earl" had been intercepted, it was obvious to both prosecution and defense alike that the solid front presented by the Gondola Girls in the first trials was about to split wide open. As the trial unfolded, Knight did his best to prepare the jury for the anticipated appearance of Ruby, who had been missing since early 1933, as a witness for Patterson.

Leibowitz provoked Victoria into admitting that she had been married twice before, first to a Henry Presley and then to one Ennis McClendon. However, she insisted on calling herself Mrs. Price for reasons best known to herself. When Leibowitz suggested that the presence of semen in her vagina might have been the result of some shenanigans in a hobo jungle just outside of Chattanooga the night before the freight ride, she screamed, "You can't prove it!" But, in the main, Knight was successful in blocking most questions concerning Victoria's previous condition of rectitude or her sexual activities on the nights of March 23 and 24.

After Dr. Bridges, Lee Adams, Orry Dobbins and Tom Taylor Rousseau had repeated their 1931 stories, Knight called Art Woodall who had previously testified that he had found Victoria's penknife in Norris's pocket. Now, he insisted that he couldn't remember which Negro had the knife, but whoever it was had told him that he had taken it "from one of the white girls." When it was shown to Mrs. Price, she immediately identified it as hers and swore that it had been held against her throat during the rapes. This testimony so delighted the attorney general that he couldn't refrain from applauding the witness and had to be taken from the courtroom to regain his composure.

All of the defendants except Norris, Weems and Roy Wright took the stand. Knight threw their previous admissions at them but each one now insisted that, not only had he not attacked any white girls, he had also not seen any other defendant do so. Any incriminating statements they had made at Scottsboro had been beaten or extorted from them. As Patterson put it, "We was scared and I don't know what I said. They told me if we didn't confess, they'd kill us, give us to the mob outside." They were followed by Dr. E. E. Reisman, a Chattanooga gynecologist, who said that much of Victoria's testimony about her physical condition did not coincide with what one would expect to see in a woman who had been violently raped six times. Dr. Bridges had previously admitted that the most he could "say about the whole case is that both of these women showed that they had intercourse."

Lester Carter said he had first met Victoria when they both were inmates of the Huntsville Jail. He confirmed that he and Tiller had spent two nights with the girls in a hobo jungle and that he had boarded the freight with them on the morning of March 25. He and the other six boys who had been in the gondola had been held in custody in Scottsboro during the first trials but had never been called as witnesses by the prosecution.

Then the bailiff called out the name of Ruby Bates. Shortly after the interception of her "Dearest Earl" letter, the ILD had sent her to New York City for safekeeping. There she had stayed with Dr. Harry Emerson Fosdick, who had urged her to return to Alabama and testify on Patterson's behalf. Once the hubbub in the courthouse had died down, Leibowitz went straight to the point.

> Q. You testified at each of the trials at Scottsboro, didn't you?
> A. Yes.
> Q. You said you saw six Negroes rape Victoria Price and six raped you, didn't you?
> A. Yes, but I was excited when I told it.
> Q. You told at Scottsboro that one held a knife at your throat, and what happened to you was just the same that happened to Victoria Price. Did someone tell you to say that?
> A. Victoria Price told me to say that. I said it like she told me to.
> Q. Did she say what would happen if you didn't do as she told you to?
> A. Yes, she said we might have to lay out a sentence in jail.

Bates freely admitted that she had lied at the first trials because

"Victoria… said we might have to stay in jail if we didn't frame a story for crossing the state line with men… every time she said 'rape' I did not know what rape was."

After the prosecution harangued the 12 Sand Mountain farmers in the jury box with warnings about "justice… bought and sold in Alabama with Jew money from New York," they retired at 12:45 p.m. on April 9, 1933. Twenty-two hours later their foreman handed a piece of paper up to Judge Horton. On it, in large, laboriously printed letters, was Patterson's death warrant. "We find the defendant guilty as charged and fix the punishment at death in the electric chair." One week later, Horton set June 16 as execution day.

Patterson was returned to the Jefferson County Jail pending a decision by Judge Horton on a motion filed by Brodsky on April 16 asking for a new trial because the conviction was against the weight of the evidence. In the interim, Knight prepared to try the case of Charlie Weems and asked Horton to call it for trial. But the judge refused to do so, feeling as he did that statements made by both Leibowitz and Knight had contributed to the "already heated atmosphere which surrounds this case." Back in New York, Leibowitz was referring to the jury as "those bigots whose mouths are slits in their faces, whose eyes popped out at you like frogs, whose chins dripped tobacco juice, bewhiskered and filthy…" Knight was no less effusive in voicing his opinion of "Jew justice." Accordingly, Horton decided to adjourn Weems's trial "until such time when in [his] judgment a fair and impartial trial may be had."

But the biggest surprise of all was yet to come. On June 22, Horton announced that he had decided to grant Brodsky's routine motion for a new trial. Not only did he disbelieve Victoria Price's testimony, but he felt that the other evidence in the case "preponderates in favor of the defendant." His 108-page opinion (which was to cost him his job at the next November elections) clearly indicated that he had not believed a word that Victoria had said. "The conclusion becomes clearer and clearer," he wrote, "that this woman was not forced into intercourse with all of these Negroes upon that train, but that her condition was clearly due to the intercourse that she had had on the night previous to this time."

On November 20, 1933, Patterson went back to Decatur for his third trial. This time the judge was William Washington Callahan, who, according to Patterson, was "the toughest, most freckle-faced, bald-headed man I was ever up against." After Leibowitz tried to show that seven Negro names now found on the jury roll had been forged, the principal actors went through their dreary lines again and, on December 1, Patterson was convicted for the third time. When Callahan imposed the death sentence, he forgot to include the customary prayer for mercy. Perhaps even God was tired of reruns.

A week later, Norris was also convicted and the two men were sent back to Kilby's death house. On June 28, 1934, Alabama's highest court affirmed the convictions and Leibowitz and Pollak promptly appealed to the U.S. Supreme Court. On April 1, 1935, Chief Justice Charles Evans Hughes announced that both convictions had been reversed because Negroes had been barred from grand and petit jury duty in Jackson and Morgan Counties. The immediate result was that the Jackson County Grand Jury returned new indictments for rape against all nine boys. But something new had been added: for the first time in as far back as Alabamans cared to remember, a Negro — one Creed Conyer — sat on a grand jury.

Haywood Patterson's fourth trial began on January 20, 1936, before Judge Callahan again. The Scottsboro Defense Committee, which was a composite of all the organizations that had been involved in the case, was now running operations and Leibowitz took the long trek south again. But the years didn't seem to make much difference as far as Morgan County juries were concerned and Patterson was convicted once more. This time he was sentenced to 75 years in prison. After the Alabama Supreme Court affirmed his conviction, the ninth jury to listen to Victoria's tale of woe found Norris guilty and he was sentenced to death. Andy Wright was then sentenced to 99 years and Charlie Weems to 75 years. Ozie Powell pleaded guilty to assaulting a deputy sheriff and was given 20 years in state prison.

On July 24, 1937, after Weems and Powell were sentenced, "the Scottsboro prosecution staff" announced that the charges against Roy Wright, Olen Montgomery, Eugene Williams and Willie Roberson were being dropped. "...After careful examination of the testimony, every lawyer connected with the prosecution is convinced that the defendants Willie Roberson and Olen Montgomery are not guilty." As for Roy Wright and Eugene Williams, charges were being dropped. "After careful examination of this crime, one of these juveniles was 12 years old and the other one was 13... the ends of justice would be met at this time by releasing [them] on condition that they leave the state, never to return."

Negotiations for the release of the remaining five went on during the rest of 1937. On December 21, Governor Bibb Graves told three members of the Scottsboro Defense Committee that he agreed that, if four of the defendants were not guilty, the remaining five were equally innocent. "The position of the State is untenable, with half out and half in on the same charges and evidence," he told them.

"The position of the State is untenable, with half out and half in on the same charges and evidence."
–Governor Bibb Graves

"When the cases come before me, I intend to act promptly." After 10 months of technicalities, Graves agreed to release all the imprisoned defendants, with the exception of Ozie Powell, to the Defense Committee on Monday, October 31, 1938. However, on October 29, he wired the committee that he was forced to postpone their release.

It was not until January 8, 1944, that Alabama decided to open the gates of Kilby Prison to Andy Wright and Clarence Norris. A few months later, Charlie Weems followed them through "the little green gate" to the outside world. Ozie Powell was paroled on June 16, 1946 and, two years later, Patterson escaped from prison and fled to Michigan where Governor Mennen Williams refused extradition. He died of cancer on August 22, 1952 in a Michigan prison where he was serving a term for manslaughter. Although Norris was picked up in 1944 as a parole violator, he was finally released on September 26, 1946. Andy Wright suffered the same fate in 1946 but gained his freedom a year later and was last heard of in 1954 when he was picked up in Albany, New York, for slashing his wife with a butcher knife.

Perhaps the saddest episode of all occurred on August 16, 1959, when Roy Wright, the youngest of the Scottsboro Boys, shot and killed his wife in New York City because he thought that she had been unfaithful to him. He then committed suicide and was found dead on the floor of his Harlem apartment with an open Bible by his side. According to Mrs. Bill (Bojangles) Robinson, who, with her husband, had raised him after Leibowitz had brought him north: "he made it a point through his life since he came here to keep good company and to keep away from anything that might get him into trouble. He didn't want his background on the Scottsboro thing hashed over again."

The Rosenbergs
The United States of America v. Julius Rosenberg, Ethel Rosenberg and Morton Sobell

No political trial in U.S. history has engendered and sustained the controversy and passion as that of Julius and Ethel Rosenberg and Morton Sobell. New and exculpatory evidence has emerged since the Rosenbergs were electrocuted; since Sobell began serving a 30-year sentence in 1953 and since Bill Kunstler wrote his trial analysis 10 years later.

With the help of the skilful attorney Marshall Perlin, the Rosenbergs' sons, Robbie and Michael Meeropol, brought a Freedom of Information Act (FOIA) lawsuit. They sued the FBI, the CIA, the Atomic Energy Commission, and the Justice, State and Defense Departments for information relevant to their parents' case. These agencies refused to release all the files for reasons of "national security" and withheld hundreds of thousands of pages. Nonetheless, in a dogged 10 year effort new information was pried from them. Summaries of the findings demonstrate unequivocally that:

1) The FBI and prosecution manufactured trial testimonies, contrived evidence and held joint meetings with key witnesses during which time the witnesses were drilled, coached and coerced into conforming and corroborating their testimonies.
2) The trial judge, Irving R. Kaufmann, who became Chief Judge of the Circuit Court of Appeals, violated the U.S. Criminal

Code, the Code of Judicial Conduct and the U.S. Constitution by:
a) holding secret one-sided ex parte meetings and communications with the prosecution and the FBI before and during the trial;
b) committing himself, before the jury had rendered a verdict, to imposing the death penalty on the Rosenbergs;
c) interfering with and attempting to influence appellate review of the case, which included scrutiny of his own conduct as trial judge;
d) deciding, before reading defense papers and hearing defense arguments, to deny post-conviction motions; and attempting at least until 1975 to use the FBI and other agencies of the government to stifle and deter inquiry into and dissent relating to the case.
3) The U.S. Government engaged in massive, illegal electronic and physical surveillance, mail covers and openings, manipulation of "friendly" press and media, and suppression and stifling of critical or questioning publicity.

Previously unavailable papers on the Rosenberg case were released by the National Security Agency in 1995. There were 49 decoded Soviet intelligence messages that were said to have been transmitted between the United States and the Soviet Union between 1943 and 1945, which were intercepted by the U.S. Army under a secret program called Venona. The messages were decrypted between 1947 and 1952, a year before the twin executions and the sending of Sobell to Alcatraz prison. Cover names were given to individuals, organizations and locations. Writing in the *Nation* in August 1995, Walter and Miriam Schneir, prominent scholars of the Rosenberg/Sobell case, wrote:

> The initial release of decoded documents includes almost everything available on the Rosenberg case or atomic espionage, according to NSA historian David Hatch. What the messages show, briefly, is that Julius Rosenberg was the head of a spy ring gathering and passing non-atomic defense information. But the messages do not confirm key elements of the atomic spying charges against him. They indicate that Ethel Rosenberg was not a Soviet agent. And they implicate the American Communist Party in recruitment of party members for espionage.

But were the Venona documents reliable? After all that had happened, should the U.S. Government be trusted? Kunstler thought not. In a letter to the *Nation* dated August 1, 1995, written shortly before his death, he wrote:

Walter and Miriam Schneir's anguished repudiation of their oft-expressed view that the Rosenbergs were "unjustly convicted" and "punished for a crime that never occurred" ("Cryptic Answers," *Nation*, August 14/21), is said to be based on alleged decoded Soviet intelligence messages just released by the National Security Agency. It is a classic example of the childlike faith of most Americans in the credibility of officialdom. They assume that the materials are authentic, and then conclude that as writers whose "duty... is to tell the truth," they must declare that the documents prove that Julius Rosenberg was a Soviet spy, albeit on an extremely minor level.

Writers also have a duty to refrain from jumping to swift conclusions, and to ask relevant questions in their search for the truth. For example, if the documents reveal that, as late as the end of 1944, Ethel Rosenberg "was not a Soviet agent," a fact certainly known by the FBI by 1953, how could any government permit her to be executed as one? Again, since many of the intercepts were decoded before the couple's arrests, why was there no apparent surveillance of their activities during that period?

Having so quickly accepted the authenticity of the 49 intercepts between the KGB and Soviet consulates in New York and San Francisco, the Schneirs rush to buttress their integrity as investigative reporters. Barely two weeks after the release of the Soviet messages, they leapt into print to declare the truth of their content. I have long respected them and consider them to be my good friends, but I wish they had waited for the dust to settle at least a little longer before their quick retreat.

Morton Sobell was released — unrepentant and unbowed — from prison after serving 18 years. In his introduction to the second edition of his autobiography *On Doing Time* written in March 2000, Sobell wrote:

At the initial press conference to mark the public opening of the Venona decryptions all guns were trained on proving the guilt of Julius Rosenberg, and the news headlines the following day universally reflected this. According to the NSA, Venona offered definitive proof of Julius's guilt. Oddly enough, even though every effort was made to identify me in Venona, I could not be found in any of the 2,200 decrypted cables. Initially, I was tentatively identified in three of the cables under the code names "Rel" and "Serb," but in the end this was acknowledged to be a mistake since, according to a subsequent cable, Rel/Serb had an artificial leg. I initially accepted the decryptions as true, but found the correlation between the cover names in the cables and the true names suspect, since the NSA refused to reveal the methods used to make the connections. Subsequently I stumbled on evidence that the decryptions promulgated by the NSA were not true decryptions, but rather, cobbled-together fictions made with the help of the FBI and its files. My request to see the initial decryptions, made before the FBI got into the act, was denied on the grounds of security, although this material is now more than 50 years old. I now have a suit pending against the NSA in an effort to force them to reveal these initial decryptions, which would demonstrate the extent of their fictionalizing.

Ethel was arrested five weeks after Julius for the purpose of applying pressure on him to confess. Julius always maintained his innocence, writing at the time that their trial was a "political frame-up through which they paraded perjured stool pigeons and professional witnesses." FBI Director J. Edgar Hoover had a phone placed in Ethel's death row cell in order to get her to denounce Julius. Yet she went to her death with a calmness and dignity that astounded witnesses. In their final letter to their sons Robbie and Michael, the Rosenbergs wrote:

> Your lives must teach you too, that good cannot really flourish in the midst of evil; that freedom and all the things that go to make up a truly satisfying and worthwhile life must sometimes be purchased very dearly. Be comforted, then, that we were serene and understood with the deepest kind of understanding, that civilization has not yet progressed to the point where life did not have to be lost for the sake of life; and that we were comforted in the sure knowledge that others would carry on after us.

Michael Smith

Early on the evening of Wednesday, September 5, 1945, Igor Gouzenko, an obscure 26-year-old cipher clerk from the Russian Embassy in Ottawa, walked into the editorial offices of the *Ottawa Journal* with an armful of secret Soviet files. When the Canadian authorities, with Gouzenko's help, translated the 109 documents he had pilfered, they discovered that the country was honeycombed with Russian spies who were part of an extensive network that covered Great Britain, the United States and Canada. Perhaps the most important name that was found in the Gouzenko papers was that of Allan Nunn May, a British atomic scientist, who was then working at the Montreal Laboratory of the National Research Council. It was through Dr. May's efforts that, on August 9, 1945, Colonel Nicolai Zabotin, the Russian Embassy's military attache, was able to report to Moscow that he had obtained samples of Uranium 233. May was

arrested when he returned to England in late September and, after
pleading guilty to a charge of violating the Official Secrets Act, was
sentenced to 10 years in prison.

The secret service agents who examined Dr. May's papers had
found the name "Fuchs" scrawled on several pages of notes. For
some reason, no attention was paid to this name although Dr. Klaus
Emil Julius Fuchs, a German-born physicist who was a naturalized
British subject, had just returned to England from a tour of duty with
the Manhattan Project, the U.S. atomic bomb station at Los Alamos,
New Mexico. It wasn't until four years later that Fuchs was arrested,
and immediately confessed that he had been supplying atomic information to a Soviet courier who regularly visited him in New York and
New Mexico. He did not know the name of the courier but indicated
that he had appeared to have an excellent knowledge of chemistry.

When he was shown photographs of various U.S. chemists who
were suspected of espionage, he had pointed to one and said, "That
is the man!" The photograph he had identified was that of a bio-
chemist named Harry Gold who was employed by the Pennsylvania
Sugar Company in Philadelphia. It was Gold, Fuchs said, who had
met him in various parts of the United States and to whom he had
turned over certain information for transmission to Anatoli A.
Yakovlev, a Russian diplomatic agent in New York. He had first met
Gold in Woodside, Queens, in June of 1944, and continued these clan-
destine meetings until he was transferred to Los Alamos early in 1945.

Upon his apprehension, Gold admitted that he had been working as a Soviet espionage agent for more than 15 years. He had first
met Yakovlev, a long-nosed young man who walked "with somewhat
of a stoop" and who was known to him only as "John," in March of
1944, at a Manhattan restaurant. Yakovlev had ordered him to contact Fuchs, who was then working in New York with a British-U.S.
atomic team. At the Woodside meeting, the physicist had told Gold
that he was "going to give me information. This information was to
relate to the application of nuclear fission to the production of a military weapon." A few weeks later, the two men had met in Brooklyn's
Borough Hall area where Fuchs gave the courier "a package of
papers" for transmittal to Yakovlev.

Just before Fuchs left for Los Alamos in February of 1945, Gold
saw him in Cambridge, Massachusetts. In addition to the usual package of documents which he had turned over to Gold, Fuchs "made
mention of a lens which was being worked on as a part of the atom

bomb." Before the two parted company, they made a date to meet in Santa Fe in June. When Gold told Yakovlev about the lens, the Soviet agent "was very agitated and told me to scour my memory clean so as to elicit any possible scrap of information about this lens."

Four months later, Gold and Yakovlev met in Volks' Cafe on 42nd Street and Third Avenue. After the details about meeting Fuchs in Santa Fe had been discussed, Yakovlev told Gold that, on the same trip, he would also have to visit Albuquerque where he was to see a U.S. soldier named David Greenglass who was stationed at Los Alamos. He was to tell Greenglass, "I come from Julius" and show him a piece of cardboard from a dessert box. "Yakovlev told me that the man Greenglass... would have the matching piece of cardboard." Either Greenglass or his wife would have some information for him and he was given an envelope containing $500, which he was to turn over to them. Yakovlev told him that he would find the Greenglasses in an apartment at 209 North High Street.

On June 2, 1945, Gold, after seeing Fuchs, took a bus from Santa Fe to Albuquerque. About 8:30 that evening, he went to the High Street address that Yakovlev had given him but was informed by a neighbor that the Greenglasses were not home. Early the next day — a Sunday — he returned to High Street and this time found the couple in their apartment. After informing Greenglass that he "was from Julius," Gold produced the piece of cardboard which matched that in the other man's possession. Greenglass, who was "a young man of about 23 with dark hair," then introduced Gold to his wife, Ruth, and asked him to come back later that day as the information was not yet ready for delivery. That afternoon, Greenglass gave Gold "an envelope which he said contained... the information on the atom bomb." Before Gold took his leave, Greenglass informed the courier that he expected to come to New York on furlough around Christmas and that "if I wish to get in touch with him then I could do so by calling his brother-in-law Julius and he gave me the telephone number of Julius..."

Gold returned at once to New York and turned over the material he had received from Fuchs and Greenglass to Yakovlev. Although he returned to New Mexico again in September of 1945 to see Fuchs, he never saw the Greenglasses again. Fuchs told him that the first atomic bomb had been exploded at Alamogordo in July and that he thought that "he would probably very soon have to return to England." The scientist was extremely upset because the British had entered Kiel ahead of the Russians and he was afraid that his Gestapo dossier would fall into the wrong hands. Gold told him not to worry and that, after his return to England, he would be contacted on the first Saturday of every month at the Paddington Crescent station of the London subway. He was to carry five books in one hand and two in another, while the man who would meet him would have a copy of Bennett Cerf's *Stop Me if You Have Heard This* in his left hand.

When Gold was apprehended on May 23, 1950, he told his story to the FBI agents who had picked him up. As a result of his revelations, David Greenglass and his wife, Ruth, were arrested three weeks later in their New York City apartment. Like Gold, the Greenglasses confessed that they, too, had been engaged in espionage activities on behalf of the Soviet Union. They insisted, however, that they had merely been pawns in the hands of Julius Rosenberg, an electrical engineer, who was married to David's sister, Ethel. It was Julius, they both claimed, who, with assistance from Ethel, had persuaded them to become atomic spies and who had directed their espionage activities. On July 16, the Rosenbergs were arrested in their 11th-floor apartment in Knickerbocker Village, a middle-income housing project on Manhattan's lower East Side.

One month later, the Federal Grand Jury in New York returned conspiracy indictments against Julius Rosenberg, Ethel Rosenberg and Anatoli Yakovlev. Four weeks earlier, Harry Gold had pleaded guilty to the same crime in Philadelphia and been sentenced to 30 years in prison. On October 10, 1950, a superseding indictment included David Greenglass and an electrical engineer named Morton Sobell as additional defendants. They were all accused of conspiring to deliver to "a foreign nation... documents, writings, sketches, notes and information relating to the National Defense of the United States of America." Since Yakovlev had returned to Russia in December of 1946 and David Greenglass had admitted his guilt, another indictment which named only the Rosenbergs and Sobell was filed on January 31, 1951, and their joint trial began in New York City on March 6, 1951.

When court convened at 10:30 that morning, District Judge Irving R. Kaufman, a comparative newcomer to the Federal bench, presided. Irving H. Saypol, the U.S. Attorney for the Southern District of New York, and five assistants appeared for the government. The Rosenbergs were represented by a father-son team — Alexander Bloch for Ethel and Emanuel H. Bloch for Julius. Harold

M. Phillips and Edward Kuntz stood up for Sobell while O. John Rogge, the attorney for the Greenglasses, only hung around long enough to ask Judge Kaufman to notify him when his client took the stand so that he "could be in attendance." The judge assured him that he would be happy to do so and Rogge, with a grateful smile, double-timed out of the courtroom.

After a jury of one woman and 11 men had been impanelled, Saypol called Max Elitcher, a former employee of the Navy Department's Bureau of Ordinance. Elitcher had attended Stuyvesant High School and City College with Morton Sobell. He said that Sobell had taken him to a Communist Party get-together in the fall of 1939 and that he had then regularly attended such meetings. In 1941, Sobell had left Washington to study for his Master's degree at the University of Michigan.

Three years later Elitcher, who had remained with the Navy Department, received a telephone call from "a person who said he was Julius Rosenberg," a former City College classmate, and who, like Sobell and Elitcher, was an electrical engineer. This man had visited him that same day and asked him whether he would be willing to obtain "classified information about military equipment" and turn this over for transmittal to Russia. He had assured Elitcher that his old friend Sobell was "helping in this way." Before the two parted, Rosenberg instructed the witness to telephone him as soon as he had any information so that it could be promptly photostated and returned to the Navy Department before it was missed. Elitcher told him that he "would see about it."

On Labor Day, the Elitchers joined Sobell and his fiancé on a vacation trip to Kumbabrow State Park in West Virginia. When Elitcher mentioned Julius's visit, Sobell appeared agitated and said, "He should not have mentioned my name." Elitcher tried to pacify him by pointing out that Rosenberg "knew about our close relationship [and] probably felt safe about it," but Sobell kept insisting, "it makes no difference, he shouldn't have done it."

A few months after Sobell's marriage in March 1945, the Elitchers spent a night in New York at the Rosenbergs' apartment. The latter announced that he had been discharged by the Signal Corps for security reasons. According to Elitcher, "he thought it had to do with his espionage activity, but he was quite relieved to find out it only had to do with the party activity." He next saw Rosenberg in September when Julius came to Washington and dropped in for "15 or 20 minutes." The conversation was limited to Elitcher's work on fire control devices for the Navy. Rosenberg asked him whether he "would want to contribute [to satisfy] a continuing need for new military information for Russia," and Elitcher testified that "I said I would see and if I had anything and I wanted to give it to him, I would let him know."

Meanwhile, Sobell had left Ann Arbor for Schenectady where he was employed by General Electric. Elitcher visited him there early in 1946, only to be pumped about the availability of written reports on the Navy fire control system. When he told Sobell that, "it was not completed, it was dragging along, it had not been finished yet," he was advised to see Rosenberg as soon as possible. Some months later, he met Rosenberg again in his Knickerbocker Village apartment. This time Rosenberg complained that "there was a leak in this espionage" and that it would be better if "I don't come to see him until he lets me know or until someone informs me." In fact, Julius thought that things were so hot that he ordered Elitcher to discontinue his Communist Party activities until further notice.

In 1947, Sobell left General Electric and took a job as a project engineer with the Reeves Instrument Corporation in New York. From time to time, Elitcher visited him at the plant and, toward the end of the year, had lunch with him at a restaurant on Third Avenue known as the Sugar Bowl. During the meal, he remembered that his ex-roommate had "inquired as to whether I knew of any engineering students... who would be safe to approach on this question of espionage, of getting material." Elitcher claimed that he knew of nobody who fitted this bill but "if somebody came along, I would tell him about it."

After several meetings with Sobell at Reeves, Elitcher made up his mind to leave the Bureau of Ordinance and enter private industry. In June 1948, during a business trip to New York, he telephoned Sobell to inform him of his plans, and the former told him not to take any final step "before you see me. I want to talk to you about it, and Rosenberg wants to speak to you about it." Later that day, Elitcher met Rosenberg and Sobell at 42nd Street and Third Avenue. They did everything in their power to persuade Elitcher to stay in the Bureau because, as Julius put it, "he needed somebody to work at the Navy Department for this espionage purpose." During this conversation, Sobell kept repeating, "Julie is right; you should do that." But Elitcher was adamant and, after the three men had dinner together, returned to Washington to resign from the Navy Department and bring his family back to New York.

At this time, Sobell lived at 164/17 73rd Avenue in Flushing. Elitcher was successful in landing a job at Reeves and, in late July, drove to New York on an apartment-hunting expedition. While driving through Baltimore, he noticed that he was being followed by several cars. When he arrived at Sobell's house that evening, he told his friend that one or two cars had tailed him during most of his northward trek. Sobell was furious. "At this point, he became very angry and said that I should not have come to the house under those circumstances." After he calmed down, he told Elitcher that he had something in the house "that he should have given to Julius Rosenberg some time ago…" He said he was tired and asked Elitcher to join him on the 10 mile trip to Manhattan. As they were leaving the house, Elitcher "saw him take what I identified then as a 35-millimeter film can."

The two men left Queens and drove down the East River Drive to the Journal-American Building where Sobell parked the car. He took "this can out of the glove compartment" and, after instructing Elitcher to drive the car around the corner and wait for him on Catherine Slip, walked off in the direction of Knickerbocker Village. When he returned some 30 minutes later, Elitcher asked him, "Well, what does Julie think about… my being followed?" Sobell assured him that "it is all right; don't be concerned about it," and headed the car in the direction of Flushing. As they drove along, Sobell volunteered the information that Rosenberg had told him that he once spoke to Elizabeth Bentley on the telephone but that "he was pretty sure she didn't know who he was and therefore everything was all right."

Before Saypol turned the witness over to the impatient defense quartet, he had extracted the information that Sobell had "a Leica camera, and an enlarger and material for processing film." Elitcher was sure that Sobell had worked on classified material when he was employed by the Navy, General Electric and Reeves. He had last seen his friend in June of 1950 when Sobell and his family left for a weekend in Washington.

Q. Did he say anything to you at that time about going to Mexico?
A. No.

Only the uninitiated in the courtroom were ignorant of the fact that Sobell had been picked up in Mexico City in the late summer of 1950 by Mexican security police and rushed across the Rio Grande.

On cross-examination, Elitcher conceded that he had signed a loyalty oath in 1947. "I signed a statement saying that I was not or had not been a member of an organization that was dedicated to overthrow of the government by force and violence."

> Q. At the time you verified that oath, did you believe that you were lying when you concealed your membership in the Communist Party?
> A. Yes, I did.
> Q. So you lied under oath?
> A. Yes.

When he was first questioned about the Sobells and the Rosenbergs, he "realized what the implications might be" of his perjured statement. But he insisted that he "didn't know what would happen to my skin when I told the story. I certainly have hopes... that the best will happen to me."

With the witness's admission that he had been going to a psychiatrist since 1947 because of marital difficulties, the defense attorneys let him go. There was bigger game in the offing. The bailiff called out the name of David Greenglass and, accompanied by a U.S. Marshal, the ex-sergeant walked up to the witness chair. Although Elitcher had testified to a connection between Sobell and Rosenberg and some suspicious activities by both men, he had not shown that either one was engaged in atomic espionage. This was David Greenglass's function and he played his role to the hilt.

After being trained as a mechanic at the Haaren Aviation School, Brooklyn Polytechnic and Pratt Institute, Greenglass was drafted in April of 1943. When he finished basic training, he had been sent to ordinance school at Aberdeen, Maryland. In July 1944, he was assigned to the Manhattan District Project at Oak Ridge, Tennessee. After two weeks orientation, he was sent to Los Alamos where he worked in the "E" shop as a machinist. He was one of 10 machinists in the shop and became its foreman some 18 months later. But it was not until November 1944 that he learned that the work he was doing was "concerned with the construction of the atom bomb."

It was his wife, Ruth, who had enlightened him as to the nature of the Manhattan Project. On November 29, 1944 — their second wedding anniversary — she visited him in Albuquerque. A few days after she arrived, the couple decided to walk to the Rio Grande via Route 66. It was during this outing that Ruth told her husband that the Rosenbergs had invited her to dinner just before she left New York. Ethel and Julius had informed her that they had become Soviet espionage agents and that they were "giving information to the Soviet Union." Julius had then told Ruth that David "was working in the atomic bomb project at Los Alamos and that they would want me to give information to the Russians."

At first, David refused to help the Rosenbergs, but, after a night of soul-searching, he apparently had a change of heart. The next day, he furnished his wife with the code names for such scientists as J. Robert Oppenheimer, Neils Bohr and George B. Kistiakowski as well as information about "the general layout of the Los Alamos Atomic Project, the buildings, number of people and stuff like that." Ruth told her husband that she had been instructed by Julius "not to write it down, but to memorize it." Two days later, she returned to New York.

Greenglass next saw his wife on New Year's Day of 1945 when he arrived home on a 15-day furlough. Julius came over one morning and "asked me to give him information, specifically anything of value on the atomic bomb, whatever I knew about it." He was particularly interested in some high explosive lens molds on which David told him he was working at Los Alamos. That evening, Greenglass drew some sketches of the lens molds, and gave them to his brother-in-law the following morning. In order to assist Greenglass in preparing his sketches, Julius gave him "a description of the atom bomb" of the Hiroshima type.

Two or three days later, the Greenglasses were invited to dinner at the Rosenbergs'. There they met a woman by the name of Ann Sidorovich. Later that evening, Julius told David that Mrs. Sidorovich would go west during Ruth's next trip to Albuquerque and that the two women would exchange pocketbooks in a Denver movie theatre. Ruth's was to contain the latest information on the atom bomb that David would turn over to her in Albuquerque.

However, there was a chance that another courier would be sent. To make sure that the Greenglasses would be able to identify Sidorovich's replacement, Rosenberg gave Ruth one part of the side of a Jello box and told her that whoever came to Albuquerque would have the other portion. Ruth put the piece of cardboard in her wallet. The rest of the evening was spent in discussing lenses, and Rosenberg told Greenglass that "he would like me to meet somebody who would talk to me more about lenses." The person Julius had in mind was a Russian scientist and an appointment was made for David to meet this man a few nights later on First Avenue between 42nd and 59th Streets.

Greenglass borrowed his father-in-law's Oldsmobile and parked at the spot Julius had indicated. His brother-in-law brought over a strange man who got into the car and ordered David to drive around the area. He asked the machinist a great many questions about lenses — the high explosive used, the means of detonation and the formula of the curve in the lens. David promised to find out what he could when he returned to Los Alamos and he drove the Russian back to where he had entered the car. He then returned home where "I told my wife where I had been."

Two weeks later, he returned to the Manhattan Project. Early the next April, Ruth joined him in Albuquerque. Shortly after she arrived, the couple found an apartment at 209 North High Street. David managed to spend Saturdays and Sundays at the apartment, returning to the base on Monday mornings. It was on one of those Sundays — June 3, 1945 — that Harry Gold made the first of his two visits to the Greenglasses. After announcing that he came from Julius and exhibiting the other half of the Jello box side, he was told by David to come back later as the information was not yet ready. As he left the apartment "Mrs. Greenglass told me that just before she had left New York City to come to Albuquerque, she had spoken with Julius..."

That afternoon, David turned over to Gold several sketches of a lens mold, some descriptive material about atomic bomb experimentation, and a "list of possible recruits for espionage." He also indicated that a test explosion was scheduled for July at Alamogordo, New Mexico. The Greenglasses then accompanied the courier on a back road that led by the USO where "we dropped him. We went into the USO, and he went on his way. As soon as he had gone down the street my wife and myself looked around and we came out again and back to the apartment and counted the money."

Q. How much was it?
A. We found it to be $500.
Q. What did you do with the money?

A. I gave it to my wife.

It was at this point that Saypol introduced a sketch of a lens mold, which had been prepared from memory by Greenglass after his arrest. The latter stated that it was, for all practical purposes, a replica of one he had given Gold in Albuquerque.

In September, Greenglass arrived in New York on furlough. He stayed at his mother's apartment on Sheriff Street where Rosenberg visited him the next morning. Greenglass told him, "I think I have a pretty good description of the atom bomb." He turned over a sketch and some data relating to the bomb to his brother-in-law who seemed delighted with them. He gave David $200 and told him that "he would like to have it immediately, as soon as I possibly could get it written up..." A replica of this sketch was identified by an atomic engineer at a later stage of the trial as a cross-section of "the bomb we dropped at Nagasaki, similar to it."

That afternoon, Greenglass typed some 12 pages of information and then drove over to Knickerbocker Village with Ruth where he gave the manuscript to Julius. The latter insisted that the report's grammar be corrected and Ethel retyped it on a portable in the living room. While this was going on, Julius told David that he had once stolen a proximity fuse when he worked for the Emerson Radio Company. Before the Greenglasses left that afternoon, Julius advised David to stay at Los Alamos as a civilian when he was discharged from the army.

David received an honorable discharge at Fort Bliss in El Paso on February 28, 1946. He immediately returned to New York where he went into business with his brother Bernard, Julius Rosenberg and a man named Goldstein. The four formed two companies — G & R Engineering and the Pitt Machine Products Corporation. Some time in 1946 or 1947, Julius urged David to continue his schooling at Russian expense "for the purpose of cultivating the friendships of people that I had known at Los Alamos and also to acquire new friendships with people who were in the field of research that are in those colleges, like physics and nuclear energy." He suggested a number of institutions, including the University of Chicago, the Massachusetts Institute of Technology and New York University, but Greenglass "never bothered" to go.

In August of 1949, David left Pitt and G & R and got a job with the Arma Engineering Corporation. In the three years he had been working with his brother-in-law, Julius had told him a great deal about his espionage activities. According to Greenglass, Rosenberg was receiving information from General Electric as well as from someone in Cleveland, Ohio. "He told me that he had people going to school in various upstate institutions." In 1947, he revealed that he had heard "from one of the boys" about a sky-platform project, and information about "atomic energy for airplanes" from another. As a reward for all his varied activities, he informed David, he and his wife had been given watches, a citation and a console table by the Russians.

Q. Did he describe the citation at all?
A. He said it had certain privileges with it in case he was sent to Russia.

A few days after Klaus Fuchs's arrest in February 1950, Rosenberg awakened Greenglass one morning and insisted that he accompany him on a walk around nearby Hamilton Fish Park. He told David that the man who had visited him in Albuquerque five years before had been one of Fuchs's contacts and that he would probably be picked up soon. He urged Greenglass to leave the country and promised to obtain some money for him from the Russians. For the next few months, Rosenberg kept pressing David to get out of the United States but it was not until Harry Gold's arrest in May that he told him, "you will have to leave the country."

At that time, he gave David $1,000 and promised him $6,000 more. He suggested that David and Ruth go to Mexico City and that they get their tourist visas at the border rather than at the Mexican Consulate in New York. Once the couple arrived in Mexico City, they were to make contact with the Russian Ambassador and, by following instructions that would have delighted E. Phillips Oppenheim, eventually wind up in Czechoslovakia. Greenglass went so far as to have six sets of passport pictures taken. On Memorial Day, he turned five sets over to Rosenberg who, a week later, brought him $4,000 in tens and twenties in a brown paper bag. Almost all of this money, he said, had been given to O. John Rogge as a fee for legal services.

In the days that followed this visit, David began to notice that he was being regularly followed. When Julius asked him, "Are you being followed?" he told him that he thought he was. His brother-in-law then asked him what he intended to do about it and Greenglass told him, "I am not going to do anything. I am going to sit — I am going to stay right here." On June 15, David was picked up by agents of the FBI. One month later, Julius Rosenberg was taken into custody and, on August 11, Ethel was arrested. The circle that Gouzenko had started in 1945 was full.

Ruth Greenglass told much the same story as had her husband. Julius and Ethel had persuaded her to encourage her husband to commit espionage. Her brother-in-law had given her $150 for a railroad fare when she first visited David in Albuquerque in late November 1944. A few days after she arrived, she and her husband took a stroll out of Albuquerque on Route 66 and she "told him that Julius was interested in the physical description of the project at Los Alamos, the approximate number of people employed there, whether the place was camouflaged, what the security measures were, and the type of work that David himself did..." The next day, after consulting "with memories and voices in my mind," Greenglass told her what she wanted to know and, when she returned to New York a few days later, she wrote it all down for Julius who seemed "very pleased."

She said that the plan to switch pocketbooks with Ann Sidorovich in a Denver theatre had soon been abandoned in favor of a meeting in an Albuquerque supermarket. On March 3, 1945, she left New York for her second trip to Albuquerque where, after three weeks of apartment-hunting, she found the place on North High Street. On April 18, she suffered a miscarriage and immediately wrote to Ethel Rosenberg to tell her that she was confined to bed and would be unable to keep the supermarket rendezvous which had been scheduled for "the last Saturday in April or the first Saturday in May." Ethel wrote back that "a member of the family would come out to visit me the last weeks in May, the third and fourth Saturdays." The Greenglasses visited the Central Avenue Safeway, which had been chosen as the meeting spot, on both Saturdays but "no one came." It wasn't until Sunday, June 3, that Harry Gold walked into their living room and announced that he came "from Julius."

Her description of the Gold visit was similar to David's except that she insisted that her husband had taken the Jello box side out of her wallet while, as he remembered it, it had been in her purse. The remainder of her testimony pertaining to the various acts of espionage that took place during the rest of 1945 did not differ materially from her husband's. She did recall a conversation with Ethel in 1946 about a "mahogany console table" which her sister-in-law told her "she had gotten... as a gift." Julius interrupted to say that, "it was a special kind of a table" and pointed out that its underside had been hollowed out so that it could be used for micro-filming.

The defense made a monumental effort to discredit both wit-nesses. The spectacle of a brother testifying against his sister was not a pretty one and Emanuel Bloch made the most of it.

> Q. Do you bear any affection for your sister Ethel?
> A. I do.
> Q. You realize, do you not, that Ethel is being tried here on a charge of conspiracy to commit espionage?
> A. I do.
> Q. And you realize the grave implications of that charge?
> A. I do.
> Q. And you realize the possible death penalty; in the event that Ethel is convicted by this jury, do you not?
> A. I do.

But David insisted that he had always loved his sister "as far back as I ever met her and knew her." If his testimony hurt her, he was sorry, but he felt "remorse" and had to get it off his chest.

Bloch also tried to show that Greenglass lacked the technical knowledge necessary to understand the material he said he was obtain-ing for Julius. David admitted that he had failed all eight courses he had taken at Brooklyn Polytech, that he had never obtained a degree in science or engineering, and that he had had no training in nuclear or atomic physics. As far as the army was concerned, he was classified as an automotive machinist and a toolmaker. What he did know about the bomb, he had "picked up here and there."

As far as the Blochs were concerned, the Greenglasses were testi-fying against their clients in the hopes of avoiding punishment for their participation in the espionage conspiracy. At the time of the trial, Ruth had neither been arrested nor indicted despite the fact that she had been very much a part of Rosenberg's plans. Bloch pumped David about this.

> Q. Now, Mr. Greenglass, your wife has never been arrested, has she?
> A. She has not.
> Q. And she has not pleaded guilty to any conspiracy to commit espionage, has she?

A. She has not.

Q. And your wife is at the present time home taking care of your children; isn't that right?

A. That's right.

His father tried the same tack when he had Ruth on the stand. She had stated that, after her husband's arrest, she had informed her lawyer, O. John Rogge, that she wanted to testify for the government.

Q. Well, was it your state of mind that you thought you would not be punished?

A. No, I didn't want to be punished.

Q. Did you hope not to be punished?

A. I did.

Q. And did you at the time you spoke to Mr. Rogge, hope that, if you told the truth and your husband told the truth, you wouldn't be punished?

A. Mr. Bloch, I have always hoped that...

Q. Will you answer my question, please?

A. Yes.

Bloch Jr.'s parting shot at the Greenglasses involved the nature of their relationship with Julius after the failure of the machine shop in 1949. Ruth testified that "we lost everything in that business." When her husband pulled out in August of that year, he had asked to be compensated for his 25 shares of stock. In fact, Ruth had "bought a book of promissory notes" and drafted several notes for her brother-in-law to sign. "We asked Mr. Rosenberg to sign the promissory notes and he refused, and he said we did not have the understanding that required it — a verbal understanding was sufficient, and he gave neither my husband nor his brother a note." But she insisted that the incident did not cause any friction between the two families even though she had consulted Mr. Rogge about David's rights.

Q. Well, aren't you a bit angry with either Mr. or Mrs. Rosenberg because they did not pay you what you think you were entitled to?

A. I don't think I am angry. I just can't understand their actions because there was a debt due.

Q. You are not angry?

A. No, I am not angry. I don't understand people who do not pay their debts, Mr. Bloch.

Q. And you resent it?

A. I don't think I resented it. I couldn't understand why I wasn't being paid for what was rightfully mine.

It was David's recollection that he had assigned his stock to his sister's husband in January 1950 but that it hadn't been turned over to him until late April. There was some discussion about the price to be paid for the stock — David wanted $2,000 but finally agreed to accept half that amount in the form of a note. After he gave the stock to Julius, he claimed that Rosenberg never signed the promissory note which Ruth had prepared for him. When Greenglass was arrested, he asked Rogge to start a law suit against Rosenberg for the "few thousand dollars" he said he had lost in the machine shop venture. When Ruth testified, she swore that David had never asked his lawyer to sue Julius — "I was the one who spoke of it," she insisted, "not my husband."

The Greenglasses were followed on the stand by Harry Gold, whose apologia included the saga of his trip to Albuquerque in June 1945. His version of the episode was identical with those previously put into the record by David and Ruth. He had arrived in Santa Fe on Saturday, June 2, where he had a 30-minute conversation with Fuchs. He then took the bus to Albuquerque, a 60-minute run, where he "managed to obtain a room in the hallway of a rooming house." Early the next morning, he had registered in his own name at the Hilton Hotel and then walked to the North High Street address Yakovlev had given him, and climbed "a very steep flight of steps" to the Greenglasses second-floor apartment. Although Ruth and David had testified that they did not receive the $500 from Gold until his afternoon visit, the courier remembered that he had given them the envelope containing the money that very morning.

Because Gold, other than by his references to "Julius," did not implicate either the Rosenbergs or Sobell, he was not cross-examined by the defense team. As he vacated the witness chair to return to the Lewisberg Federal Penitentiary, Saypol called Dr. George Bernhardt. Bernhardt was a physician who lived only a few doors away from the Rosenbergs on Monroe Street. He recalled a telephone conversation he had had with Julius in May 1950. According to him, the defendant had said, "Doctor, I would like to ask a favor of you. I would like to know what injections one needs to go to Mexico." When the doctor demurred, Julius had assured him that "it is not for me; it's for a friend of mine." Bernhardt then told him that he would need "typhoid injections and a small-pox vaccination."

During this conversation, Bernhardt informed Rosenberg that if his friend was a veteran "all he would need would be booster doses instead of going through the entire series of injections, and Rosenbergs said, 'Yes, he is a veteran.' " He told his caller that the typhus injection would not be necessary, however, if his friend was going only to Mexico City but Rosenberg said, "He will probably go into the interior." Then, Bernhardt had recommended, "if he decided to go... give me a little notice because I don't usually stock a typhus vaccine and I would have to get it, and he said he would let me know."

> Q. Did that complete the conversation you had with him?
> A. That is right.

Bernhardt admitted to Bloch Jr. that he had been treating Julius for hay fever during May 1950. Rosenberg used to come to the physician's Knickerbocker Village apartment once a week for injections. These injections were usually given in Bernhardt's living room. But the witness couldn't remember whether he had ever discussed vacations with his patient or shown him pictures he had taken on Cape Cod. He was certain, however, that he had never discussed "with Julius Rosenberg his taking a vacation in Mexico."

The government got back to the subject of Morton Sobell again with the testimony of William Danziger, another City College graduate who had worked with him in the Bureau of Ordinance. Danziger had left Washington in March 1950 to take a job with the Academy Electrical Products Corporation in New York. Shortly after his arrival, he had looked up the Sobells and, with his wife, visited them in Flushing. It was during this visit that Sobell, after learning that his guest was in "the electrical business," had suggested to him that he might be able to use Rosenberg's machine shop.

In the latter part of June, Danziger visited the machine shop where he was informed that Julius was "out at a stamping place. I was at that time rather interested in getting an estimate on stamping, so I went out to the stamping place and saw him out there." In July, Danziger dropped in at the shop once more "to look over the... facilities." Rosenberg told him that, "he was rather tied up at that time" and would be unable to accept any new work "for some months." If Danziger wanted some work done, he was advised "to contact him some time in the future."

On June 20, Danziger telephoned Sobell and told him that he was looking for an electric drill in order to do some repair work at his home. Sobell informed him that "he was getting ready to leave for a vacation in Mexico," but if Danziger wanted a drill, he would have to come to Flushing to get it. When he arrived at the Sobell apartment that evening, he noticed that "there was packing going on, there were valises standing there." He also saw a car in the driveway with some valises in it. After Sobell gave him the electric drill, he told Danziger "he was going to Mexico City by air."

Some weeks later, Danziger received a letter addressed to him at the Academy Electrical Products Corporation from an "M. Sowell" in Mexico City. It was from Sobell and contained two enclosures that he was asked to "forward... and I will explain to you when I get back." One was a note to Sobell's parents and the other to Edith Levitov, a sister-in-law who lived in Arlington, Virginia. Danziger delivered both notes and also followed Sobell's directions to "deliver my address to Max Pasternak."

Q. Did you know who Max Pasternak was?
A. I knew he was related in some way.

In the middle of July, he received a second letter from Mexico City. This time, the name on the envelope was "M. or Morty Levitov." It contained "a letter for me, an enclosure for Miss Edith Levitov and a short additional note which he asked me to forward, using somewhat similar phraseology, 'I will let you know about it when I get back.' " Danziger promptly forwarded the note to Miss Levitov and never heard from Sobell again. Before he stepped down, the witness said he thought that the return address on the second communication — a Cordova or Corbova Street — was different from the one on the first envelope.

Then a Mexico City interior decorator with the impressive name of Manuel Giner de Los Rios sauntered up to the stand. With an interpreter at his side, he testified in a soft Spanish that he lived in Apartment Five at 153 Calle Octava de Cordoba. He remembered that the Sobells had rented Apartment Four at the beginning of July 1950, and that he had had a conversation on the stairs with Morton about a tank of cooking gas on the day they moved in. A week later, he invited the new tenants to "a party for the family and friends in honor of the saint's day..."

The Sobells soon reciprocated by inviting de Los Rios and his wife to dinner. A few days afterwards, Sobell, who appeared to be "a little nervous, a little worried," asked his new friend "how one could leave Mexico."

> Q. Did he make any statement as to why he wanted to leave Mexico?
> A. Only because he was afraid.
> Q. Did he say specifically what he was afraid of?
> A. He was afraid that they were looking for him so that he would have to go to the army.
> Q. Did he say who was looking for him?
> A. The military police.

"Sometime around the July 20 or 22, 1950," de Los Rios recalled, Sobell had gone to Vera Cruz where he stayed "for about 15 days." The decorator had received two letters from him during this period, both of which began with the salutation, "Dear Helen." The first was postmarked Vera Cruz and the second was from Tampico. He delivered each letter personally to Mrs. Sobell.

The interpreter had his work cut out for him that afternoon. Señor de Los Rios had no sooner left the courtroom when the bailiff called out the name of Minerva Bravo Espinosa, who, it turned out, worked in an optical shop on the Calle Cinco de Mayo in Vera Cruz. On July 26, 1950, a U.S. citizen who gave his name as "Mr. M. Sand," had placed an order with her for a pair of glasses. She had no difficulty in recognizing Sobell as that man. He had filled out a card "which purchasers make out to specify what they buy." At this point, Mr. Kuntz stood up and announced that, "we will concede that we filled out the card and used the name of Sand and bought a pair of glasses there."

Jose Broccado Vendrell, who was one of the proprietors of the Grand Hotel Diligencias in Vera Cruz, remembered that a "Morris Sand" had stayed at his establishment until July 30.

Vendrell was followed by Dora Bautista, a clerk at a Tampico hotel. On July 30, a American, who gave his name as "Marvin Sand," had registered and asked her for directions to the Banco Granadero. Both witnesses identified Sobell as the man they had seen. Glenn Dennis, an official of a Mexican airline, confirmed that a passenger by the name of "M. Sand" flew from Vera Cruz to Tampico on July 30, and a "Morton Solt" from Tampico to Mexico City two days later.

Elizabeth Bentley, fresh from her triumphs before sundry congressional investigating committees, contributed little to the prosecution's case. Outside of adding to the aura of communism that permeated the entire trial, her testimony consisted only of innuendo. In the fall of 1942, she had accompanied Golos, her party superior (and lover), to the vicinity of Knickerbocker Village, where he was "to pick up some material from a contact, an engineer." At that time, she had waited in a car while Golos talked to his "contact." From then until November of the next year, she used to receive telephone calls from a man "who described himself as 'Julius.' " Golos had told her that this man "lived in Knickerbocker Village," but she had "never met anyone whose voice I heard, whom I could describe as Julius."

The government's last witness was James S. Huggins, an immigration inspector for the Justice Department. On August 18, 1950, nine Mexican security policemen had brought Morton Sobell to his office in Laredo, Texas. He identified a manifest record which he had filled out from information given to him by Sobell. At the bottom of the card, he had written, "Deported from Mexico," despite the fact that the Mexican authorities had not shown him any deportation orders. As soon as Huggins had laboriously typed in the necessary personal data on the manifest, the defendant was arrested by FBI agents who were waiting in the outer office.

As Huggins left the witness stand and headed back for the anonymity of the Immigration and Naturalization Service, Saypol announced that "the government rests, if the court please." In a little less than two weeks, the prosecution had presented the evidence that it hoped would convict all three defendants. After some defense motions for a mistrial because of the infusion of testimony about the Communist Party were denied, Bloch, Jr. informed Kaufman that, "my first witness is the defendant Julius Rosenberg."

It was late on the afternoon of March 21, 1951, that the mustached, bespectacled Rosenberg sat himself down in the witness chair. A 33-year-old electrical engineer, he proudly stated that he had married Ethel on June 18, 1939, and that they were the parents of two boys, Michael and Robert. Outside of the fact that he knew a great many people whose names were mentioned during the trial, he denied that he had in any way been involved in espionage. As for Russia, he "felt that the Soviet Government had improved the lot of the underdog there... and at the same time I felt that they contributed a major share in destroying the Hitler beast who killed six million of my coreligionists."

> Q. Did you feel that way in 1945?
> A. Yes, I felt that way in 1945.
> Q. Do you still feel that way today?
> A. I still feel that way.

But he was, and always had been, loyal to the United States.

He testified that Greenglass had asked him for $2,000 in May of 1950. When Julius asked him why he needed this money, he was told, "I need the money. Don't ask questions." David had also urged his brother-in-law to see if his doctor "would make out a certificate for a smallpox vaccination." In addition, he had wanted to know "what kind of injections are required to go into Mexico." It was after this conversation that Rosenberg had questioned Dr. Bernhardt about the medical requirements for a Mexican trip.

Toward the end of May, David had telephoned Rosenberg and pleaded with him to come over to his apartment. He told Julius, whom he usually called Julie, that he was "in a terrible jam." He said he needed a "couple of thousand dollars in cash" and, when his brother-in-law told him that he couldn't raise that amount of money, he had shouted, "…if you don't get me that money you are going to be sorry!" Outside of an inconsequential meeting a few days later, that was the last time that Julius had seen David until the latter testified at the trial.

Ethel buttressed her husband's emphatic denials of any espionage activities. She knew that Julius had purchased their console table at Macy's and that "it was about $20 or $21." Long after the trial, such a table, which a Macy employee priced at $20 to $36, was found in her mother-in-law's apartment. As far as wristwatches were concerned, the one she had been wearing when she was arrested had been given to her by her husband on her birthday in 1945. She remembered that Julius had lost his watch on a New York Central train in August 1948. She was certain that neither the console table nor the watches had been given to them by the Russians.

When Saypol took over, both witnesses refused to answer any questions that had to do with their association with the Communist Party. Julius informed Judge Kaufman that "if Mr. Saypol is referring to the Young Communist League or the Communist Party, I will not answer any question on it…"

Q. You mean you assert your constitutional privilege against self-incrimination?
A. That's right.

Ethel bridled at any reference to the word "communist" and refused to answer such questions as "Did you ever sign a Communist Party nominating petition for elective office?" and "Were they [friends with whom the Rosenbergs had lived for a time] members of the Communist Party?"

After Thomas V. Kelly, a Macy's attorney, testified that it was impossible to check the purchase of the console table because the store's records for 1944 had been destroyed, the defense called it a day. But Saypol had three rebuttal witnesses up his well-tailored sleeve — Evelyn Cox, a domestic who had worked for the Rosenbergs in 1944 and 1945; Helen Pagano, a legal secretary employed by O. John Rogge and Ben Schneider, a commercial photographer. Mrs. Cox was there to swear that Ethel Rosenberg had once told her that the console table had been given to her husband as "a sort of a wedding present." Mrs. Pagano said that Louis Abel, who was married to Ruth Greenglass's sister, had brought $3,900 to Rogge's office on June 16, 1950, the day after David's arrest, and that this money had been wrapped "in a brown bag." Schneider identified the Rosenbergs as the couple who had ordered some passport pictures from him on a Saturday in May or June of 1950.

On March 29, the jury, after deliberating for more than 18 hours, returned verdicts of "guilty as charged" against all three defendants. One week later, Judge Kaufman sentenced the Rosenbergs to death because, as he somewhat awkwardly put it, "...your conduct in putting into the hands of the Russians the A-Bomb... has already caused, in my opinion, the communist aggression in Korea with the resultant casualties exceeding 50,000..."

As for Sobell, Kaufman thought that "the evidence... did not point to any activity on your part in connection with the atom bomb project" and sentenced him to 30 years, the maximum prison term provided by the Espionage Act, with a "gratuitous" recommendation that he never be admitted to parole. The next day, David Greenglass, whose sentence had been deferred to the end of the trial, was sentenced to a 15-year term.

After more than two years of fruitless appeals and motions for a new trial, the Rosenbergs' executions were set for 11:00 p.m. on the night of June 19, 1953, at Sing Sing Prison. Three days before, Irwin Edelman, "an interested citizen," filed a motion with Mr. Justice William O. Douglas, in which he argued that the penalties of the Atomic Energy Act rather than those of the Espionage Act were applicable and that, under the former, the Rosenbergs could not have been sentenced to death. On June 17, Douglas granted a stay of execution in order to give Edelman's attorneys time to argue their point. But Chief Justice Vinson reconvened the court on the following day and the full bench, by a six-to-three vote, vacated Douglas's stay at noon on June 19. After President Eisenhower refused to grant clemency, the couple's execution was moved ahead three hours in order to avoid a conflict with the Jewish Sabbath. A few minutes after 8:00 p.m., Julius and Ethel Rosenberg passed into what Joseph Conrad once called "the great indifference of things."

After President Eisenhower refused to grant clemency, the couple's execution was moved ahead three hours in order to avoid a conflict with the Jewish Sabbath. A few minutes after 8:00 p.m., Julius and Ethel Rosenberg passed into what Joseph Conrad once called "the great indifference of things."

Engel, Education and God

Steven Engel, Daniel Lichtenstein, Monroe Lerner, Lenore Lyons and Lawrence Roth v. The Board of Union Free School District Number Nine

Like Scopes's case in Tennessee, this case centers on the First Amendment to the U.S. Constitution, which mandates the separation of church and state. It prohibits federal or state governments, and their agencies, from making any law "respecting an establishment of religion," meaning that governments are prohibited from requiring any form of religious observance. Many cases decided by the Supreme Court have tested this prohibition. An area that has been particularly contested is prayer and religious instruction in public schools. Until recently, most efforts to bring prayer, the Bible or God into public schools have failed; the Supreme Court has struck them down. The court prohibited the mandatory reading of at least 10 verses of the Bible at the beginning of the school day; it struck down a requirement that schools post the 10 commandments in classrooms; it found prayer at school assemblies to be unconstitutional and ruled that clergy could not lead prayer at graduations.

The key Supreme Court case upon which these ruling are based, decided in 1958, is *Engel v. Vitale*, which Bill Kunstler so eloquently describes. The case concerns a 22-word prayer to "Almighty God," appealing for God to bless the country, its parents and its teachers. School students were initially required to say the prayer, although this was later modified — allowing them to remain silent if their parents made a written request to the school. The prayer requirement was mandated in 1951, at a time when the United States was engaged in its cold war against a so-called "Godless communism" — and forcing children to say the prayer was probably seen as a way of "immunizing" them against communism.

The Supreme Court found that the use of public schools to promote prayer violated the First Amendment's prohibition against laws establishing any religion. Even though the saying of the prayer was "voluntary," the court pointed out that the government itself had written the prayer and was encouraging students to say it. One of the questions asked by the court of a lawyer defending the prayer, was whether he would defend it if it had been an Islamic prayer. The lawyer said he would not, because such a prayer would not reflect the spiritual heritage of the United States. That answer must have sunk any real support for the prayer — demonstrating its religious origins and the fact that it was a prayer for some and not for others.

An important aspect of Bill Kunstler's story of the case is the courage of those who were willing to stand up for the First Amendment and take the case to court. They, and their children, were unceasingly harassed and threatened. It became even worse for the plaintiffs after the case was won. Those who wanted prayer in schools saw the ruling as supportive of communism and picketed the house of plaintiff Lawrence Roth, bearing signs that read: "FBI, investigate Mr. Roth! Impeach the pro-red Supreme Court." Many politicians and religious leaders of the time spoke out against the court's decision. Yet despite these objections, and efforts to amend the U.S. Constitution, the *Engel* ruling remained the law of the land.

Engel remains law today, although the current Supreme Court has already begun to restrict its meaning. The court recently refused to rule on a challenge to a state law, currently enforced in Virginia, requiring that students observe a daily minute of silence; the law says the student, "may meditate, pray or engage in any other silent activity." The court also ruled that schools could not prohibit religious clubs from meeting on their premises after school, if nonreligious clubs could also meet. In addition, as of this writing in May 2002, the court is considering whether governments can issue vouchers that can be used to pay tuition at religious schools.

The Supreme Court even considering such a case would have been unheard of just a few years ago.

The attacks of September 11 have brought an upsurge in efforts to bring God and religion into schools. Teachers in some schools are handing out "In God We Trust" buttons; "God Bless America" signs are sprouting up in classrooms; and ministers are addressing school assemblies. In Congress, a new effort is underway to amend the constitution to allow school prayer. Named the "School Prayer Amendment," it had no chance of passage prior to September 11, and while it is still unlikely to pass, its chances have most certainly increased.

The struggle for a secular education in schools, that Bill Kunstler describes so well and that occurred over 40 years ago, still continues today. Those who fought this battle must be remembered, and their courage set as an example for all of us.

Michael Ratner

In the fall of 1951, the Board of Regents of New York State University, which included members of the three major religious faiths, unanimously adopted a 22-word nondenominational prayer for use in the public schools. "Almighty God," it read, "we acknowledge our dependence upon Thee and we beg Thy blessings upon us, our parents, our teachers and our country." In recommending the prayer to local school districts, the 13 regents suggested that it be recited in conjunction with the pledge of allegiance to the flag. "We are convinced," they said, "that this fundamental belief and dependence of Americans — always a religious people — is the best security against the dangers of these difficult days."

On July 8, 1958, the five-member board of education of the Herricks Union free school district in New Hyde Park, a Long Island suburban community, some 20 miles due east of New York City, by a vote of four to one, adopted a resolution "that the regents' prayer be said daily in our schools," and directed District Principal Lester Peck "that this be instituted as a daily procedure to follow the salute to the flag." The board's action was duly reported in *On Board,* its official bulletin, which was distributed to all taxpayers in the district. Lawrence Roth, a plastics manufacturer who had moved to Long Island from New York City seven years earlier, was one of the issue's most interested readers.

Roth, a slim, bespectacled man in his mid-40s, whose sons, Joseph and Daniel, attended two of the district's seven schools, was distressed by the board's action. Although he had been vaguely aware that there was some pressure to introduce the regents' prayer into the district's schools, he also knew that six previous attempts to do so had failed. The school board's sudden about-face caught him completely by surprise but, being what his lawyers were later to call euphemistically a "nonbeliever," Roth was deeply disturbed by the prayer's implications. His two sons, who were 10 and 13 years old, shared his religious views, and he was concerned with their spiritual and psychological reaction to the new prayer that was scheduled to start in September.

Roth began to discuss the problem with a Catholic neighbor who shared a seat with him on the commuter train to New York City which left the Long Island railroad's Albertson station at 7:03 each morning. It wasn't long before the plastics manufacturer realized that his knowledge of the U.S. Constitution as it affected church-state relationships was extremely limited. When his commuter friend recommended that he contact the New York Civil Liberties Union (NYCLU), Roth called that organization at once and spoke to George Rundquist, its energetic director, who suggested that Roth drop in for a chat at his earliest convenience.

In early August, Roth, who was more uneasy than ever about the regents' prayer, arrived at Rundquist's ninth-floor office on lower Fifth Avenue. Although the latter shared Roth's doubts about the prayer's constitutionality, he pointed out that any legal action to invalidate it would almost certainly subject Roth and other parents who might join with him to strong community pressures. "You will be hated and despised by most of your neighbors," Rundquist told his caller, "and your children will have to face the scorn of many of their classmates. But if you are willing to endure all of this, I'll query our board of directors." Roth nodded his head: "I'm willing," he replied firmly. On September 4, Rundquist sent a memorandum to the members of his board at NYCLU which detailed several items on the proposed agenda for their regular monthly meeting five days later. Item 11 read as follows:

Regents' Prayer For Public Schools

The Situation:
On July 8, the school board of the Herricks Union free school district (Nassau County) voted that the school day shall be opened by recitation of the following prayer, recommended by the Board of Regents in November, 1951: "Almighty God, we acknowledge our dependence upon Thee, and we beg Thy blessings upon us, our parents, our teachers and our country."

At the time that the proposed prayer was released, the NYCLU, along with many civic organizations, expressed its oppo-

sition to reciting this prayer in the public schools through a public statement to the press and a letter to the New York City board
of education (December, 1951). We also requested that the matter be considered at a public meeting so that we might have an
opportunity to present our views on the matter.

Because of public reaction to the regents' proposal, the New
York City board of education took no action until January 15,
1953. At that time, it adopted a resolution that students sing the
fourth stanza of "America" each school day, following the pledge
of allegiance: "Our fathers' God, to Thee/Author of Liberty/To
Thee I sing/Long may our land be bright/With freedom's holy
light/Protect us by Thy might/Great God, our King."

The Question:
Should the NYCLU adhere to the policy adopted in 1951? If so,
shall we implement our position by supporting a group of residents in the Herricks school district who seek to enjoin the school
board from proceeding with the recitation of the prayer?

The 1951 letter to which Mr. Rundquist referred had been sent to
Maximilian Moss, the president of the New York City board of education. In it, John Paul Jones, then the NYCLU's chairman, had
asked for a public hearing before the regents' prayer was considered.
"Our opposition," Jones had written, "is based in law upon the ruling of the U.S. Supreme Court that neither a state nor the federal
government can set up a church. Neither can pass laws which aid
one religion, aid all religions, or proffer one religion over another.
The NYCLU believes that the proposed nondenominational prayer
falls within the ban of the First Amendment as thus interpreted by
the Supreme Court."

Jones was quick to point out that his organization had no objection to programs devoted to spiritual teaching, but that, since it was
impossible to present such programs without interpretation, they
would inevitably lead to the expression of sectarian points of view.
"Our opposition to the regents' proposal is not opposition to the
teaching of religion," he concluded. "But it is the belief of the
NYCLU that the teaching of our spiritual heritage, through prayer
and special programs, is the function of religious leaders and of parents and not the proper function of public school teachers conduct-
ing classes in public schools supported by public funds."

On September 9, Rundquist reviewed the situation for the
NYCLU's board of directors at their regular luncheon meeting at a

midtown hotel. While several of his listeners thought that it would be wiser to work through the legislature rather than the courts, the majority voted to assist Roth and Roth's neighbors with legal help. "It was moved and passed," the minutes of the meeting read, "that we reaffirm our 1951 position in opposition to the prayer and, assuming that we have counsel willing and with time to take over, that we intervene in the case."

As soon as Rundquist returned to his office, he put in a call to William J. Butler, a former staff counsel of the American Civil Liberties Union (ACLU), who had specialized in corporation law since entering private practice. Butler, a tall, stocky Harvard graduate in his mid-30s, whose four grandparents had all migrated to the United States from Ireland, and two of whose uncles were priests, was married to the daughter of Arthur Garfield Hays. An ensign in the merchant marine during World War II, he was a sailing fan who missed no opportunity to be on or near open water.

Quickly, Rundquist explained that the NYCLU had decided to support Roth. Was Butler interested in handling such a case? He was. "I consider this prayer ruling a dangerous threat to freedom of religion," Butler told Rundquist. "That is why I will take the case." Ten minutes later, Butler was talking to Roth. He had only one request to make of the plastics manufacturer. He would like a group of plaintiffs who represented a religious cross-section of the community and which contained no agnostics or atheists. "I'll do my best, Mr. Butler," Roth promised.

As soon as he returned home that evening, Roth placed advertisements in the *Roslyn News* and the *Williston Times,* asking for people who were interested in challenging the regents' prayer to contact him. Within two weeks, he had assembled the names of 50 Protestants and Jews as well as one Catholic. But it wasn't long before his list began to shrink. "We found," Roth later revealed, "that there was going to be a substantial amount of pressure and even vilification and hostility. One couple were 100 percent with us until they spoke to their minister. Then they came to me and said, 'We're still with you but our minister said this is a controversial matter and we can't join you.' " One of the project's most enthusiastic supporters quit when his employer warned him that "it was foolish to get mixed up in controversial cases." Finally, after two weeks of intensive effort, Roth was left with only four willing parents whose children would not graduate before the impending test case wound its way through the courts. (Seven years earlier, a suit challenging the reading of verses from the Bible in New Jersey public schools had been dismissed by the U.S. Supreme Court because all of the plaintiffs' children had graduated before the case reached its docket.)

In addition to Roth, the prospective plaintiffs whose names were given to Butler early in October, composed of three men and one woman. Steven Engel, a big, balding man in his late 30s, whose seven-year-old son Michael attended Searington school, was the international sales manager of a textile firm. A precise speaker, Engel was a Reform Jew. Forty-five-year-old Daniel Lichtenstein, a manufacturer's representative, had three children in the district's schools. Like Engel, he was Jewish and had emigrated to Nassau County from Brooklyn. A deeply tanned, stocky man with an outgoing personality, he was a handball and bridge expert. Paradoxically, he had served as campaign manager for Mary Harte, the school trustee who had moved the adoption of the regents' prayer, when she first ran for the board of education.

Monroe Lerner, an account executive in a Wall Street firm, was an analytical man who was not one to make any hasty decisions. Tall and balding, he had one child, seven-year-old Cynthia, who attended the Searington school. He was a member of the Ethical Culture Society. Lenore Lyons, whose husband did not share her antipathy toward the regents' prayer, was a tall, darkhaired woman with three children of school age. Easily the most attractive member of Roth's little band, Mrs. Lyons was the chairwoman of religious education at the Unitarian Church she and her family attended.

Before resorting to the courts, the prospective plaintiffs were required by law to submit a formal request to the school board asking it to rescind its July resolution adopting the regents' prayer. On December 4, a letter signed by all five parents was mailed to the school district's administration building in New Hyde Park. "We, and each of us," it stated bluntly, "hereby demand that you discontinue, or cause to be discontinued, the practice instituted for the first time at the beginning of the current school year of having a prayer said daily following the salute to the flag in all the schools of the district, and particularly the schools which our children attend." The prayer, the letter continued, was "a violation of the constitution of the United States and of the state of New York."

On January 6, 1959, Florence Alnwick, the clerk of the board of education, wrote to Butler. "As you are probably aware," she said, "the Education Law confers certain authority upon the board of education and pursuant thereto the board of education on July 8, 1958, adopted a resolution authorizing and directing the daily use of the regents' recommended prayer, to which you refer, in the schools within the district." Accordingly, she had been directed by the board of education to advise the lawyer that no further action on the subject of the prayer was contemplated.

While he had been waiting for the board's reply, Butler had not been idle. Anticipating a negative response, he had begun preparing a petition to the Nassau County Supreme Court shortly after his five plaintiffs had been selected. By the year's end, he had, with the aid of his partner Stanley Geller, finished his labors and, two days before receipt of the board's letter, the petition was verified by Roth and his fellow plaintiffs. Addressed to William J. Vitale, Jr., Philip J. Fried, Mary Harte, Anne Birch and Richard Saunders — the members of the board of education, it asked the court to direct the members "to discontinue or cause to be discontinued in the schools of said district the saying of the prayer designated as the regents' prayer."

In the main, the plaintiffs claimed that "the saying of the said prayer and the manner and setting in which it is said," violated both the federal and state constitutions. According to them, District Superintendent Peck had established a daily ritual for saying the regents' prayer. "Each morning at the commencement of each day in each school following the salute to the flag," their petition read, "the prayer is said aloud. The prayer is led by the teacher or by a student selected by the teacher with the other students joining therein. The prayer is said with hands clasped together in front of the body, fingers extended and pointed upwards in the manner of a suppliant. During the saying of the prayer, no student is permitted to leave the classroom."

On February 18, the school board served its answering papers on Butler. Represented by handsome, dark-haired Bertram B. Daiker of the Port Washington law firm Gunn, Neier & Daiker, it denied that the saying of the regents' prayer violated either the U.S. or the New York Constitutions. Moreover, it claimed that not only did the petitioners lack the power "to interfere with the saying of the prayer by the children of others under the color of judicial process or otherwise," but that their lawsuit, if successful, would be tantamount to an interference with freedom of religion.

An affidavit by William J. Vitale, Jr., the dapper president of the school board, accompanied the latter's answer. Vitale pointed out that, since the beginning of the school year, only one parent had requested that his child be excused from the saying of the prayer. In addition, no child had asked to leave the room during the prayer. As for the petitioners' claim that children had been forced or shown how to pray, this was simply not the case. "On the contrary," he said, "the principals and teachers in the school district have been directed and are following the directions that under no circumstances shall a pupil in any way be made or encouraged to join in the prayer and no teacher has instructed the pupils how they are to hold their hands or otherwise conduct themselves during the saying of the prayer."

Both as a school board member and a father, Vitale felt that the prayer was beneficial. "I am fully conscious of the need for instilling in the youth of today some recognition of the moral and spiritual values which are part of the heritage of this country and of this state," he argued. "The brief moment of prayer, by those who join in it at the opening of school each day, cannot help but remind those children, in the words of our state constitution, that by acknowledging their dependence on God, they may 'secure' the blessings of freedom granted by almighty God."

With the issue clearly joined, interest in the pending case began to develop rapidly. On February 24, 16 residents of the school district applied for the right to intervene in support of the regents' prayer. Speaking through their attorney, tall and articulate Porter R. Chandler, a former president of the Catholic Lawyers Guild, they maintained that they had sufficient interest in the retention of the prayer to be allowed to participate. Although Butler objected strenuously to their motion, it was swiftly granted by Judge Bernard S. Meyer. The intervenors' participation, however, was limited to the merits of the constitutional questions raised by the petitioners.

While they were waiting for their case to be argued, the plaintiffs had good cause to recall Rundquist's warning to Roth in September. From the time their suit became known, all five were harrassed by threatening letters and telephone calls. One caller told Roth that an organization known as the Union Street Benevolent Society was preparing to bomb his home. On many nights, the plastics manufacturer was forced to take his telephone receiver off the hook in order to sleep. "We're going to blow up your car," one gruff voice said. "Keep your eyes on your children," another warned.

On February 24, the contentions of all the parties were argued before Judge Meyer in the spacious county courthouse on Mineola's Old Country Road. It took the tall, youthful appearing judge exactly six months to reach his decision. In a 66-page opinion, he came to the conclusion the school board's resolution did not violate the federal or state constitutions. In particular, he stressed that "the recognition of prayer is an integral part of our national heritage [and] that prayer in the schools is permissible, not as a means of teaching 'spiritual values,' but because... at the time of the adoption of the First and 14th Amendments this was the accepted practice."

However, he did find fault with the board's resolution of July 8, 1958, which directed "that the regents' prayer be said daily in our schools." Because the resolution was couched in what he called "mandatory terms," Meyer ordered Vitale and his fellow board members to modify it so as "to establish a procedure whereby the parents of each child are advised of the adoption of the resolution calling for the saying of prayer, of the wording of the prayer and of the procedure to be followed when it is said and requested to indicate whether the child shall or shall not participate in the exercise." The case was remanded by Judge Meyer "to the board of education for further proceedings not inconsistent with this opinion."

At the end of his long opinion, the judge thanked all the lawyers involved "for the excellent presentation, not only in oral argument, but in the original and supplemental briefs." In closing, he referred to an 1837 opinion of the superintendent of common schools of the state of New York. "Written 120 years ago," he said, "the following statement, in the court's view, most completely conforms to the requirements of both constitutional law and reason: 'The simple rule, to exercise your own rights so as not to infringe on those of others, will preserve equal justice among all, promote harmony and insure success to our schools.' "

Ten days after Judge Meyer's decision, the school board took steps to comply with the latter part of his order. In a brief regulation, teachers were directed to refrain from commenting "on participation or nonparticipation in the exercise." In addition, children whose parents had submitted written requests to the principals of their schools were "to be excused from participating or from the room during the prayer exercise." Five days later, each parent in the district received a letter from District Principal Peck. After setting forth the prayer, Mr. Peck informed his addressees that "any parent or guardian who does not wish his child to say the prayer is requested to write a letter to the principal of the school his child attends, indicating whether he wants his child excused from the room or to remain silent while the prayer is being said."

In October, Butler appealed to the appellate division of the Supreme Court. During the year that intervened before the case was finally argued before the five-judge court, the school board asked Judge Meyer to dismiss the proceeding on the merits. According to Philip J. Fried, who, on July 1, had succeeded Vitale as the board's president, Peck's letter to the district's parents fully complied with Meyer's decision and there was no longer any reason for delaying the inevitable. Meyer bowed to Fried's inescapable logic. On March 17, 1961, he stated: "It appears to the court that the respondent has complied with the directions contained in the opinion of this court in the proceeding dated August 24, 1959. It is ordered that this proceeding be and is dismissed on the merits."

In opposing the board's motion, Roth et al. claimed that Peck's letter did not cure the fundamental defects involved in the saying of the regents' prayer. "Petitioners maintain," they said, "that the saying of the so-called 'regents' prayer' in the schools at the direction of and under the auspices of the board of education, violated the constitutions of both this state and the United States... The matter of the prayer is not within the cognizance of the board and should not have been remanded to respondents for further action... No actions taken by respondents on remand could have cured the fatal defects in the saying of the prayer. Indeed, petitioners submit that any actions taken by respondents since remand constitute an additional violation or additional violations of the state and federal constitutions."

On October 17, the appellate division refused to disturb Judge Meyer's ruling. Four of the judges agreed fully with Meyer's opinion. Associate Justice George J. Beldock, however, although in favor of retaining the school prayer, minced no words in declaring that he did not subscribe to the lower court's reasons for denying the petition. In particular, he found fault with Meyer's rationale that he was sustaining the prayer because it was "the accepted practice" before the adoption of the federal constitution. As far as he was concerned, the prayer was not religious training and, therefore, was not prohibited by the constitution. This, he concluded, is what Judge Meyer should have stated in no uncertain terms.

On May 25, 1961, Butler, Chandler and Daiker journeyed to Albany to appear before the Court of Appeals, New York's highest tribunal. There, together with attorneys for the Board of Regents and the American Jewish Committee, they argued the pros and cons of the school prayer issue. Six weeks later, Chief Judge Charles S. Desmond, speaking for himself and four of his colleagues, affirmed Meyer's decision. In a brief opinion, he stated that a belief in God, "has been maintained without break from the days of the Founding Fathers to the day of the inauguration of President Kennedy."

He insisted that the regents' prayer did not in the least infringe on the rights of minorities. "Belief in a supreme being is as essential and permanent a feature of the U.S. governmental system," he emphasized, "as is freedom of worship, equality under the law and due process of law. Like them it is an American absolute, an application of the natural beliefs on which the republic was founded and which in turn presuppose an omnipotent Being." Although he was uncertain as to the eventual success of the prayer service, he heartily approved of the motives of both the regents and the Herricks school board.

But, for the first time since the case had started its long, tortuous climb up the judicial ladder, there was a dissent. Two of the seven judges, Marvin R. Dye and Stanley H. Fuld, agreed with Butler's contention that the prayer was unconstitutional. "In sponsoring a religious program," they said, "the state enters a field which it has been thought best to leave to the church alone. However salutary the underlying purpose of the requirement may be, it nonetheless gives to the state a direct supervision and influence that overstep the line making the division between church and state and cannot help but lead to a gradual erosion of the mighty bulwark erected by the First Amendment." For this reason, Dye and Fuld felt that the school board should have been ordered to discontinue the use of the regents' prayer.

The way was now clear for Butler to ask the U.S. Supreme Court to consider the case. On October 4, 1961, he filed a petition for a writ of certiorari, a necessary prerequisite to an appeal. Two months later, in a brief order, the nine justices granted the writ. Three years, two months and 25 days after the board of the NYCLU had voted to support Roth, the case, which was now officially known as No. 468 of the high court's October term, 1961, had finally reached Washington.

Oral arguments in the Supreme Court's stately first-floor courtroom took place on April 3, 1962. In addition to the points raised by Butler, Daiker and Chandler, the attorneys general of 17 other states joined Roger Foley, Nevada's chief legal officer, in a brief which urged Chief Justice Earl Warren and his eight colleagues to see to it that "we shall ever remain a religious people" by sustaining the regents' prayer. The Synagogue Council, the American Jewish Committee, the Anti Defamation League of B'nai B'rith and the American Ethical Union joined Butler in asking for a reversal of the lower court decisions.

The latter commenced his argument by reciting the regents' prayer. "What's wrong with that?" interrupted Justice Harlan.

"There's nothing wrong with that," Butler replied. "We have no objection to the prayer as such. I have come before this court to defend, not attack religion. Our objection is to the use of public facilities for religious purposes."

Frankfurter, who was destined to be disabled by a paralyzing stroke three days later, broke in. "I want you to be perfectly candid with me, Mr. Butler," he piped. "Do you think the public school system should be secularized?" The lawyer thought for a moment. "Yes, I do," he responded, "because, on balance, the threat to religious freedom is so great that I would rather have secularization than the state in the business of religion."

Justice Brennan had one question. Did Mr. Butler think that there was any distinction between teaching religion and teaching about religion? He did. "The first is objectionable," he said. "The second is the duty of the state." Potter Stewart asked whether there was any difference between the prayer and the salute to the flag. Butler didn't hesitate. "There certainly is," he replied. "The prayer is a religious utterance and the salute a political one."

During Daiker's presentation, Warren wanted to know whether the school board's attorney considered the regents' prayer a religious exercise. "No, I do not," the lawyer replied. "It is merely an expression of the spiritual heritage of our nation, that the Founding Fathers believed in God." The chief justice smiled. "I would expect you to take that position," he commented wryly. Black had one question for Chandler. Would he have had any objection to the prayer had it been a Mohammedan one? "I would, your Honor," he answered. "A Mohammedan prayer does not reflect the spiritual heritage of this country."

Monday, June 25, 1962, was the last decision day before the

Supreme Court adjourned for the summer. It also marked the end of Associate Justice Hugo L. Black's 25th consecutive term of court. In a brief ceremony before attending to his crowded calendar, Warren commended Black for his long service. "Of the 97 justices who have been appointed to the court," he observed, "only 16 have served as long as Mr. Justice Black and none with greater fidelity or singleness of purpose. His unflagging devotion has been to the constitution of the United States." Black, who apparently had not been informed in advance of the intended tribute, slumped in his seat as the chief justice spoke.

The prayer ruling was the first of 17 to be announced by the court. Authored by Black, the 15-page majority opinion came to the conclusion that New York's use of the public school system to encourage recitation of the regents' prayer was "wholly inconsistent" with the First Amendment's stricture against any law "respecting an establishment of religion." "The constitutional prohibition against law respecting an establishment of religion," Black wrote, "must at least mean that in this country it is no part of the business of government to compose official prayers for any group of the American people to recite as a part of a religious program carried on by government." Accordingly, the judgment of the Court of Appeals was reversed by a vote of six to one. (Justices Frankfurter and White took no part in the decision, the former being ill and the latter having just been named to the court by President Kennedy.)

His opinion finished, Black looked up from the papers in front of him. "The prayer of each man from his soul," he said in a low voice, "must be his and his alone. That is the genius of the First Amendment. If there is any one thing in the First Amendment, it is that the right of the people to pray in their own way is not to be controlled by the election returns."

As the reporters rushed for the telephones in their basement press room, Justice William O. Douglas began reading portions of a concurring opinion which, while wholly in favor of the case's result, went much further than Black's. As Douglas saw it, the constitution prohibited any form of "religion-financing" by government. This would include chaplains in the armed forces, compulsory chapel at West Point and Annapolis, federal or state aid to parochial schools, the use of the Bible to administer oaths and the inclusion of God in the Pledge of Allegiance. "Our system at the federal and state levels is presently honeycombed with such financing," he said. "Nevertheless,

I think it is an unconstitutional undertaking whatever form it takes."

He wanted it clearly understood that his reasoning did not stem from any hostility toward religion. "The First Amendment leaves the government in a position not of hostility to religion but of neutrality," he explained. "The philosophy is that the atheist or agnostic — the non-believer — is entitled to go his own way. The philosophy is that if government interferes in matters spiritual, it will be a decisive force. The First Amendment teaches that a government neutral in the field of religion better serves all religious interests."

Mr. Justice Stewart was the only member of the court to voice a dissent. "I think the court has misapplied a great constitutional principle," he declared. "I cannot see how an official religion is established by letting those who want to say a prayer say it. On the contrary, I think that to deny the wish of these school children to join in reciting this prayer is to deny them the opportunity of sharing in the spiritual heritage of our nation." His brief opinion ended with the observation that the patriots who signed the Declaration of Independence did so with a self-styled "reliance on the protection of divine providence."

The majority decision caused an immediate reaction. George Andrews, an outraged Alabama Congressman, complained that "they put the Negroes in the schools and now they've driven God out." New York's Governor Nelson Rockefeller, who apparently hadn't read or understood Black's opinion, hoped that "adjustments" could be worked out that would make the prayer acceptable to the Supreme Court. Francis Cardinal Spellman was "shocked and frightened that the Supreme Court has declared unconstitutional a simple and voluntary declaration of belief in God by public school children." On the west coast, James Francis Cardinal McIntyre, the archbishop of Los Angeles, called the decision "positively shocking and scandalizing to one of American blood and principle."

Evangelist Billy Graham was "shocked and disappointed" by what he called "another step toward secularism in the United States." Right Rev. James A. Pike, bishop of the Protestant Episcopal Diocese of California and a lawyer himself, said that he was surprised to see that the Warren Court had extended "to an obviously nonsectarian prayer the prohibition against 'the establishment of religion,' clearly intended by our forefathers to bar official status to any particular denomination or sect." Representative John Bell Williams of Mississippi called the decision part of "a deliberate and carefully planned conspiracy to substitute materialism for spiritual values." To Senator Herman E. Talmadge of Georgia, it was "an outrageous edict which has numbed the conscience and shocked the highest sensibilities of the nation." The Alabama legislature quickly passed a resolution terming it "diabolical."

Herbert Hoover and many other prominent U.S. citizens demanded an immediate amendment to the constitution nullifying the prohibition against the prayer. "The Congress should at once submit an amendment which establishes the right to religious devotion in all governmental agencies," the former president said angrily. Representative Roy A. Taylor of North Carolina, a Baptist deacon, complied at once. His proposed amendment was as definite as it was brief. "Notwithstanding the First and 14th Amendments to the constitution of the United States," it read, "prayers may be offered and the Bible may be read in connection with the program of any public school in the United States." Senator James O. Eastland announced that the Senate Judiciary Committee would meet at once to consider proposed amendments.

But the decision was not without its supporters. Dr. Sterling M. McMarrin, U.S. commissioner of education, felt that the outlawing of the prayer was no loss to religion. "Prayer that is essentially a ceremonial classroom function," he explained, "has not much religious value." Dr. Edgar Fuller, executive secretary of the council of chief state school officers, stated that, "in my judgment, the Supreme Court is right." Senator Jacob K. Javits of New York reminded parents that there was "plenty of opportunity to inculcate religious faith in the children at home and at weekend religious schools." Rev. Dr. Dana McLean Greeley, president of the Unitarian Universalist Association, said that "the Supreme Court has acted clearly in support of the principle of the separation of church and state as guaranteed by the First Amendment of the constitution."

In Chicago, Dean M. Kelly, director of the National Council of Churches' department of religious liberty, was enthusiastic about the court's action. "Many Christians," he claimed, "will welcome this decision. It protects the religious rights of minorities and guards against the development of 'public school religion' which is neither Christianity nor Judaism, but something less than either." At his press conference on June 27, President Kennedy said that he hoped that the decision would come as "a welcome reminder to every American family that we can pray a good deal more at home, we can

attend our churches with a good deal more fidelity, and we can make
the true meaning of prayer much more important in the lives of all
of our children."

In their own area, the victorious plaintiffs were disconcerted by
the violence of the attack on the decision. Representative Frank J.
Backer, a Nassau County congressman, called it "the most tragic in
the history of the United States." William A. Bruno, a trustee of the
nearby Hicksville board of education, said that his district would
retain the prayer. "Let's see what the Supreme Court will do about
that!" he chortled. He told a reporter for the *New York Times* that the
ruling proved that Robert Welch, the founder of the Birch Society,
"had the right idea in asking for the impeachment of the Supreme
Court." Robert S. Hoshino, president of the mammoth Levittown
school district, called the decision a victory for communism.
"Levittown will not vote out the regents' prayer," he prophesized.
However, Dr. James E. Allen, Jr., the state's commissioner of education, reminded recalcitrant local school boards that they would
"have to enforce the Supreme Court decision immediately."

Although they were bitterly disappointed by the case's outcome,
both Vitale and Daiker indicated that the Herricks school board
would not disobey the Supreme Court's mandate. The former felt
certain "that any of the people involved are prepared to adhere to
the decision of the court." According to the lawyer, "the decision
must be complied with." Each man stressed the fact that no child
had been forced to recite the prayer against their will. "At no time
did we ever insist that a child should say it," Vitale declared. "We set
up procedures so no one would be compelled to say it and we felt
sincerely we were not infringing on anyone's constitutional rights."

The plaintiffs were quietly jubilant over their triumph which the
NYCLU called a "milestone" in the separation of church and state.
Lenore Lyons said that the decision represented "both liberal and
conservative thinking of the Supreme Court." Engel, Lerner and
Lichtenstein were "extremely happy." Lawrence Roth, who referred
to himself as "a very religious person but not a churchgoer," viewed
the case's result as an indication of his conviction that "religious
training is the prerogative of parents and not the duty of the state."
Butler claimed that the decision had helped rather than hindered
religion. "In this country, with its many different faiths, religion has
flourished because we have steadfastly adhered to the principle of
separation of church and state," he said. "The Supreme Court has

today reaffirmed that principle."

With the case over, Roth and his coplaintiffs revealed that, since 1959, they had been subjected to a variety of community pressures, ranging from dirty looks to abusive telephone calls. In one house, the latter had become so vituperative that the children were forbidden to answer the phone. Many of the anonymous letters and postcards that had arrived regularly at each of the five homes were obscene, anti-Semitic or both. "Toward the end, it got so bad," Roth said, "that my wife or I made it a point of getting the mail before the children could see it."

Roth's oldest son, Danny, who was now 16, said that his father's leadership of the antiprayer fight had made it very difficult for him at school. "There were arguments and pushing and name-calling," he recalled. "In the halls, kids would yell out: 'You're a commie' or 'Go home to Russia.' At times I thought it might be easier for me if my father stopped what he was doing. But I never wanted him to. I believe very strongly that what he was doing was right. I'm very proud of my father, you know."

The court's decision heightened the bitter campaign against the plaintiffs. Not only did the number of malicious telephone calls, letters and postcards increase, but Roth's house was picketed by nine members of the newly formed Nationalist Party bearing signs which read: "FBI, investigate Mr. Roth! Impeach the pro-red Supreme Court."

"The harassing phone calls got so bad Tuesday night," Roth said, "that we finally had to take the receiver off the hook again. They were coming in at the rate of two calls a minute." The anonymous callers shouted such threats as "Watch out for your child... We're going to blow up your car... Don't leave your house — something is going to happen to it... We'll get you." One postcard was typical: "To the five Long Island parents," it began. "You damn Jews with your liberal viewpoints are ruining the country."

In addition, at least one candidate in the New York primary campaigns that began shortly after the decision, in an openly anti-Semitic appeal to Roman Catholic voters in Queens County's 11th assembly district, reminded them that the school prayer had been invalidated by persons with Jewish names. "These are the names you should know," began a leaflet distributed by James E. McGinniss, an independent Democrat, "Stephen Engel, Daniel Lichtenstein, Monroe Lerner, Lenore Lyons and Lawrence Roth.

These people brought the legal action which resulted in the banning of the 'prayer' in our public schools." Mr. McGinniss then urged registered Democrats to vote for him, "if you want a public official who will remember the 'presence of God' and who will sponsor and work for laws which will permit us to live and raise our children as God-fearing citizens."

A week before the distribution of McGuinniss's fliers, the Jesuit magazine *America* chimed in with a warning "to our Jewish friends." In an outspoken editorial, the weekly reminded U.S. Jewry that, although it could not be held fully responsible for the school prayer decision, its leaders would be well advised to curb the activities of certain Jewish agencies which, the magazine claimed, hoped to secularize public life from top to bottom. "It would be most unfortunate," the editorial concluded, "if the entire Jewish community were to be blamed for the unrelenting pressure tactics of a small but overly vocal segment within it. When court victories produce only a harvest of fear and distrust, will it all have been worthwhile?"

The regents' prayer is no longer recited in the Herricks school system — or, for that matter, anywhere else in the state of New York. But it will be a long time before the five people whose efforts led to its invalidation will be permitted to forget that they ran counter to the strong feelings of their community. "Mr. Rundquist warned me of what we could expect," Roth acknowledged wryly, "but we never realized how bitter the attacks on us and our families would be. But none of us are sorry that we became involved in the case. We all feel that we have had a small part in clarifying and strengthening a vital constitutional safeguard. For this, we were more than willing to endure whatever came our way."

"We are convinced, that this fundamental belief and dependence of Americans — always a religious people — is the best security against the dangers of these difficult days."

–Board of Regents, New York State University

Epilog

In December 2001, five Cubans living in Miami were sentenced to lengthy terms of imprisonment. The "crime" of these Cubans was to monitor terrorist groups in Florida that have acted – and continue to do so – with impunity from U.S. territory against an independent and sovereign country, the small island of nearby Cuba. The five Cubans – Gerardo Hernández Nordelo, René González Sehwerert, Ramón Labañino, Fernando González Llort and Antonio Guerrero Rodríguez – have been labelled as spies, but their trials highlight the political nature of their imprisonment. They correctly claim to be political prisoners in a country that dictates to the world that all those who are not with the Empire are against it.

René González Sehwerert, one of the five Cubans who were all convicted in U.S. courts of justice, spoke the following words in his defense at trial:

"...People here have spoken with impunity against Cuba, censuring a nation of people whose only crime is having chosen their own path, and having defended that choice successfully, at the cost of enormous sacrifices...

"When Mr. Kastrenakas (lawyer for the prosecution) stood up in this courtroom, this symbol of U.S. justice, and said we had come here to destroy the United States, he showed how little that symbol and that justice matter to him...

"The evidence in this case; history; our beliefs; none of this supports the absurd idea that Cuba wants to destroy the United States. The problems of the human race cannot be resolved by destroying any country — for too many centuries, empires have been destroyed only for similar or worse empires to be built on their ruins. Threats to this nation will not come from a people like the people of Cuba, where it is considered immoral to burn a flag, whether it is from the United States or any other country.

"With the privilege of having been born here and of growing up in Cuba, I would like to tell the people of the United States not to look so far to the south to see the threat to the United States.

"Cling to the real and genuine values that inspired the founding fathers of this nation. The lack of these values, sidelined by less idealistic interests, constitute the real threat to this society. Power and technology can become weaknesses if they are not in the hands of a cultured people, and the hatred and ignorance we have seen here toward a small country, that nobody knows, can be dangerous when combined with a blinding sense of power and false superiority.

"Go back to Mark Twain and forget about Rambo if you really want to leave your children a better country. Every alleged Christian who was brought up to this courtroom to lie, after swearing on the Bible, is a threat to this country, in view of the way their conduct serves to undermine these values."

David Deutschmann

Resources

Sacco and Vanzetti

Denman Frankfurter, Marion (ed.), *The Letters of Sacco and Vanzetti*, Penguin 20th Century Classics, 1997

Avrich, Paul, *Sacco and Vanzetti: The Anarchist Background*, Princeton University Press, 1991

CD: Guthrie, Woody, "Ballads of Sacco and Vanzetti," Smithsonian Folkways, 1996

Film: Montaldo, Giuliano, "Sacco and Vanzetti," Italy, 1971

Scopes — The "Monkey Trial"

The decision holding the prohibition on teaching evolution unconstitutional is *Epperson v. Arkansas* 393 U.S. 97 (1968)

Karen Schmidt, "Creationists Evolve New Strategy," *Science 273*: 420-422, 1996-JUL-26

"*Tennessee v. John Scopes*: The 'Monkey Trial,' " at: http://www.law.umkc.edu/faculty/projects/ftrials/scopes

"Monkey Trial: Debate over creationism and evolution still with us," at: http://abcnews.go.com/sections/us/DailyNews

"State school boards grapple with evolutionary theory," Newsroom, 2001-FEB-23. See: http://www.mcjonline.com/news/01a/20010222e.shtml

The Scottsboro Nine

Carter, Dan T,*Scottsboro: A Tragedy of the American South*, 2nd Ed. Baton Rouge: Louisiana State University Press, 1984.

The Encyclopedia of the American Left, 2nd Ed. Oxford University Press, New York, 1999, p. 368

The Rosenbergs

Markowitz, Gerald E. "How Not to Write History: A Critique of Radosh and Milton's The Rosenberg File." *Science and Society 48* (Spring 1984)

Meeropol, Robert and Michael, *We Are Your Sons*, 2nd Ed. Urbana: University of Illinois Press, 1986

Schneir, Walter and Miriam, *Invitation to an Inquest*, New York, Pantheon, 1983

Sobell, Morton, *On Doing Time*, 2nd Ed. Golden Gate National Park Association, San Francisco, CA, 2000

Doctorow, E.L., *The Book of Daniel: A Novel*, Plume, 1996

rebel lives

"I am in the world to change the world."

Käthe Kollwitz

Ocean Press announces a radically new, radically refreshing series, Rebel Lives. These books focus on individuals — some well-known, others not so famous — who have played significant roles in humanity's ongoing fight for a better world. They are strongly representative of race, class and gender, and they call back from history these lives, catapulting them directly into the forefront of our collective memory.

Rebel Lives presents brief biographies of each person along with short, illustrative selections, depicting the life and times of these

"Better to die on your feet than live on your knees."

Emiliano Zapata

women and men, in their own words. The series does not aim to depict the perfect political model, visionary or martyr, but rather to contemplate the examples of these imperfect theorists, activists, rebels and revolutionaries.

Rebel Lives is produced with assistance from activists and researchers from all over the world, creating books to capture the imaginations of activists and young people everywhere. These books are smaller format, inexpensive, accessible and provocative.

Titles in preparation are:

- Rosa Luxemburg
- Sacco & Vanzetti
- Helen Keller
- Albert Einstein
- "Tania" (Tamara Bunke)
- Chris Hani
- Che Guevara
- Nidia Díaz
- Emiliano Zapata
- Haydée Santamaria

"The law
is nothing
other than a
method of
control
created by a
socioeconomic
system
determined,
at all costs, to
perpetuate itself
by all and any
means neces-
sary,
for as long as
possible."

–William Kunstler